THE COTS

SOUTHERN AREA

WALKS FOR MOTORISTS

Peter A. Price

30 Walks with sketch maps

COUNTRYSIDE BOOKS
NEWBURY, BERKSHIRE

Countryside Books' walking guides cover most areas of England and Wales and include the following series:

County Rambles
Walks For Motorists
Exploring Long Distance Paths
Literary Walks

A complete list is available from the publishers

First Published 1976
by Frederick Warne Ltd

This completely revised and updated edition
published 1991

© Peter A. Price

COUNTRYSIDE BOOKS
3 Catherine Road
Newbury, Berkshire

ISBN 1 85306 126 3

Sketch maps by the author

Cover photograph taken by Andy Williams

Publishers' Note
At the time of publication all footpaths used in these walks were designated as official footpaths or rights of way, but it should be borne in mind that diversion orders may be made from time to time.
Although every care has been taken in the preparation of this Guide, neither the Author nor the Publisher can accept responsibility for those who stray from the Rights of Way.

Produced through MRM Associates Ltd., Reading
Printed by J. W. Arrowsmith Ltd., Bristol

Contents

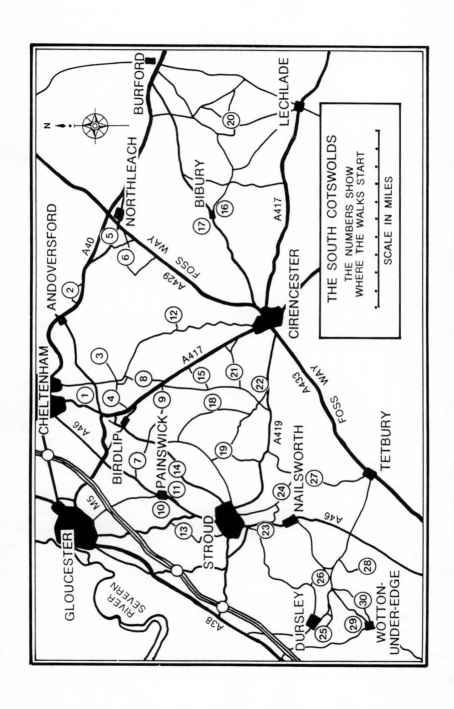

THE SOUTH COTSWOLDS

THE NUMBERS SHOW
WHERE THE WALKS START

SCALE IN MILES

Introduction

The Cotswolds is a ridge of hills which stretch from near Stratford-on-Avon in the north to Bath in the south. It is at its widest in the northern half where it is 20 miles from the Vale of Evesham in the east to Burford and the Oxfordshire plain in the west. South of the central uplands it narrows to a few miles as it approaches Bath. In the region of Stroud the steep western escarpment is cut by numerous long narrow, wooded valleys, whilst to the east of the Fosse Way it merges imperceptibly into the Wiltshire plain.

Half the walks in the South Cotswolds go through estates which are well-wooded, for the sides of the many valleys are ideal places for trees. The rich clothiers vied with each other when laying out their parks, which have now reached maturity and are more beautiful than ever their owners could have envisaged. The traveller by car who crosses the high open ground by the straight Roman roads misses the true character of the Cotswolds. It is in the by-ways and the secluded valleys that the gentle beauty of mellow buildings and the peace of leafy glades will be found.

The Cotswolds is designated as an Area of Outstanding Natural Beauty, which means it is a special type of Green Belt — it is not a National Park but a farming workshop.

The Cotswold Hills are made up of a long wedge of Oolithic Limestone, which is a type of limestone put down at the bottom of a warm, shallow sea, something like the Mediterranean, and it is not found elsewhere in the country. This provides a rich home for many plants and animals. The soil is light, well drained and alkaline. Consequently some plants are missing altogether but those preferring calcium carbonate are prolific. They include lily of the valley, thyme, basil, rock-rose, five different orchids and two helleborines, the pasque flower and the wayfaring tree. In the beechwoods it is possible to find yellow archangel, birds-nest orchid and wood melick, amongst other plants. On the western side of the Cotswolds it is unfortunate that the great variety of fungi has recently been increased to include the one responsible for the Dutch elm disease. The miles of old stone walling act as hosts to many colourful lichens. On most walks in summer one can hear the song of the chiff chaff or the goldcrest and in winter a flock of longtailed tits may flit past along the hedgerow. The hovering kestrel, working its way over the hillside is a familiar sight at all seasons of the year. Butterflies are plentiful, many of them depending on the wide variety of grasses for food.

Man has been on the Cotswolds for 9,000 years. During that time each succeeding generation has left its mark. The 'long' and 'round' barrows, the ancient straight trackways and the impressive hill forts all came before the Romans. A constant stream of invaders, some warlike, some

5

peaceful, contrived to change the face of the countryside. Some enjoyed great prosperity and left their buildings as tokens, others failed and it is necessary to look keenly to find traces of their once hopeful ventures. Each generation tends to destroy the ones which went before — but rarely do they completely succeed. A little detective work on any of these walks could unfold a fascinating story.

All walks in this book are circular, they start and finish at the same place. The routes described are on public rights of way as shown on the Definitive Map and the County Road Record, or they are on common land registered for public access. The one exception is Walk 21 in Cirencester Park, which is by permission of The Lord Bathurst. Many of the walks go through farmland or private woodland which is the source of income to the farmer. Damage to fences, walls or gates may mean suffering to animals who could get out and eat the wrong food or be injured by a car — apart from the expense involved in repairs.

Make sure you observe the Country Code:–

Guard against fire risk.
Fasten all gates.
Keep dogs under proper control.
Keep to the paths across farmland.
Avoid damaging fences, hedges and walls.
Leave no litter.
Safeguard water supplies.
Protect wild life, wild plants and trees.
Go carefully on country roads.
Respect the life of the countryside.

The most important item of equipment for the walker is footwear. You may come across quite a lot of mud even in summer, so the best protection is to have a lightweight pair of boots. Most walkers get them a size too big and then wear an extra pair of thick socks to stop them rubbing, and when turned down over the top of the boot they will stop small stones getting down under the feet. When you get back to the car you can then take them all off and change back into clean shoes. Boots are also advisable when the ground is hard and dry because the muddy gateways and tracks dry into very uneven ground and it is easy to twist an ankle in an unguarded moment.

A map is not strictly necessary if this guide is carried as the routes are described in detail and sketch maps are provided. An Ordnance Survey map, however, adds interest and helps to identify points in distant prospects that are not mentioned in the text. Such maps also show the local roads. You will find the number of the appropriate Ordnance Survey Landranger and Pathfinder Sheets which cover the area concerned, together with the map reference of the start, are given at the beginning of each walk.

On wool and cloth in the Cotswolds

There is evidence to show that some of the many Roman Villas on the Cotswolds were specialising in the production of wool. The well-drained limestone has always suited sheep and there is every reason to suppose that the large Iron Age fortifications such as those at Uley and Nottingham Hill were refuges for large flocks of sheep. But it is in the 300 years following the Norman invasion that the production and export of wool reached its peak. Sacks of wool were sent to the weavers of the Netherlands in huge quantities to be made into cloth and sold throughout Europe. During the latter part of the 14th century the export of wool declined to be replaced by the finished cloth which was to provide the prosperity the Cotswolds enjoyed for the next 500 years.

The early processes of preparing cloth depended entirely on human power, except in fulling where the large wooden hammer replaced the pounding of bare feet and the wheel on the gig-mill replaced the hand-stroking. Spinning, the most monotonous of occupations, was to remain unchanged until the late 18th century and then only came about because of the insatiable demands of the new power-looms. The industrial revolution came early to the South Cotswolds, by 1800 the 'wind of change' had been blowing for some years.

The old cottage industry — until the late 18th century

The raw wool was bought by a clothier who had it washed and dried in his own premises, which was often a small mill. It was then oiled to make it easier to work (static electricity in un-oiled wool makes it difficult to handle) and distributed to carders who combed it and spinners, both of whom worked on piece rate. The resultant yarn was then cut into lengths, called chains, for the loom. The weaver then came to the clothier to collect the chain to take home and weave on his own loom. The next stage was burling or the removal of lumps and tufts, this was craftsman's work and was done either at his home or in the mill. It was then washed and thickened in a fulling stock to remove the oil, then beaten for 12 hours with big wooden hammers and washed again. The nap was raised by teazles, at first they were set in cards and operated by hand but by 1500 a machine called a gig-mill did this mechanically. The next step was dyeing and this was done by very skilled men. The 'common' colours such as brown or olive were sometimes done at the mill but scarlet and woaded colours such as blue, black and green went to special dye-houses. Now the lengths of cloth were hung out on oak racks in the field to dry and many fields are still called 'rack close' as they were then. The final process of drawing and pressing completed 'the cloth' — a piece 26 yards long and 54 to 58½ inches wide, which was then ready for its long journey to London. On its arrival in London it went to Blackwell Hall in Basinghall Street where it was examined and stored until sold. In 1550 there were 122,000 'cloths' sent from the Cotswolds for export, all had to start their journey by road and most of them went through London.

The Factory System
During the 18th century many clothiers became rich enough to rebuild their old mills or build new ones so as to gather together all the operations of cloth-making into one place. All processes could now be mechanised and the power-loom set the pace. Soon water-power proved insufficient to meet growing demand but the canals and later the railways brought cheap coal from South Wales for the new steam engines.

By the beginning of this century almost all weaving had ceased and the oldest and perhaps the greatest industry of this country had vanished from the Cotswolds.

Many walks go through fields where mills once stood or past houses which once rang to the click of the weaver's shuttle. Some go down sunken tracks where once the train of pack-mules jostled with the cattle of the Welsh drover, or along field paths trodden by the weaver with his load of 'chain'.

Peter A. Price
June 1991

LECKHAMPTON HILL

WALK 1

★

6 miles (9.5 km)

OS Landranger 163, Pathfinder SO 81/91

Leckhampton Hill looks down over Cheltenham from the south. The walk starts from a disused quarry on the south-west side of the hill, just off a narrow lane which is signposted at neither end. GR: SO 946 177. From Cheltenham take the A46 Stroud road and ¼ mile beyond the College buildings in Cheltenham fork left on to the B4070 road to Birdlip. After climbing a long hill the road starts to wind round the hill, and on a gentle left-hand bend a narrow lane forks upwards to the left. Take this lane. From the A417 Gloucester to Cirencester road where it meets the A436 at a large roundabout near 'The Air Balloon', turn towards Cheltenham on the B4070 and in ¾ mile take the narrow lane on the right which turns back and up the hill. 300 yards up this lane on the left there is an entrance to a disused quarry. Cars can be left in here but do not park too near the face of the quarry.

Leckhampton Hill has been for many years the place to which the people of Cheltenham have walked on Sundays and Feast Days. It is now a common owned by the County Council.

Look towards the face of the quarry and turn left. Climb up one of the many small paths which go up near the entrance and then turn right. Walk along the top of the cliff for 300 yards with fine views over the valley and then take a narrow path going down to the left. This will bring you to a wall under the trees where the path winds along below the cliffs. After about ¼ mile the Devil's Chimney can be seen between the trees high up on the right as an irregular pillar silhouetted against the sky. The path eventually comes to a flat clearing in which there are strange old concrete pillars and pieces of wall. For more than 100 years until 1925 this quiet spot rang to the rumble of trucks full of stone coming from the various quarries in the hillside and going down the long incline towards Cheltenham. From here came much of the stone which built the centre of Cheltenham, its houses, its garden walls and its rockeries.

The long incline is now the main footpath from Cheltenham up to the hill. A few yards walk away from the hillside takes you to the top of the slope. Full trucks went down here pulling up the empties as they went. The 'tramroad' as it was called, went across the B4070 and down to the bottom of the hill, at one time being extended to Cheltenham and Gloucester and the trucks being pulled by horses. Return to the clearing

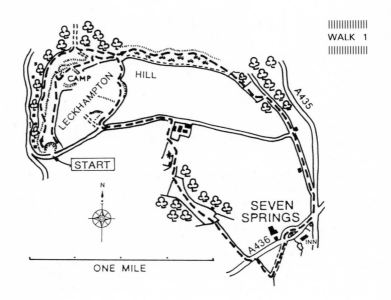

where the tram tracks from the quarries converged. The chief line came down from the left but trees now obscure its route from below.

When facing the hillside turn left and go up a path which forks after 40 yards. Take the steeper of the two paths and climb up to arrive at a junction of many paths. Opposite is a small gate in a fence. You will come back through this gate. Now turn left and go along to the top of the hill, following the arrows of the Cotswold Way. Looking over to the left you can see Cleeve Hill, the highest part of the Cotswold Hills.

Follow the path for nearly 1 mile, resisting every temptation to go down to the left. After looking down over part of the golf course the path descends with a wall on the right, through some trees into a field. Keep along the top of the field to near the far end, then go down to the bottom corner and along a track. In 200 yards continue along the lane. On reaching the A435 turn right.

Take care to keep to the wide grass verge for 75 yards before turning right along the footway of the road to Gloucester. In 100 yards bear right round the loop of the old road. Inside the loop, at the foot of the wall supporting the new road, is a small pond into which seven springs flow. On the wall is the legend — *Hic tuus O Tamesine Pater septemgeminus fons.* (Here, O Father Thames, is thy sevenfold source.) These springs are 750 feet above sea level and it is the highest point from which water flows into the Thames. It is the source of the river Churn whose waters flow further than any other before reaching the North Sea.

To continue the walk, cross the Gloucester road with care as this is a busy and fast road and walk along the verge to a narrow fenced path to the left. Go over the hill and at the cross-track turn right up the side of a field to a lay-by. Turn left for a few yards and cross the road again to a path which goes up the bank to a stile. Follow the path along the edge of a field to the corner. The stile is below field level, down on the right, and from here the path goes up a long narrow field set between woods, in the floor of the valley. This is Hartley Bottom.

Continue up the valley, bearing right round the wood to the narrow end of the field. Go over a stile on the left into the field on the left. Turn right to a gate 200 yards ahead. Pass an old pumping house on the left and continue up the valley to a point about 50 yards beyond the end of the wood on the left. Do not go on to the stile ahead next to the farm house but bear left up to a corner of the field. Go into the field and turn right, with the farmyard wall and buildings on the right, and in 200 yards come out on to a lane. Turn left along the lane and in just over ¼ mile, where the lane turns left, bear right through a narrow belt of trees. In 20 yards turn right along a track next to the trees and above the old quarry on the left.

After 300 yards it will be noticed that the track is going round the edge of a flat field. This was once the large Brown Stone Quarry but it has been refilled and returned to agriculture. At the small gate, passed on the way out, turn left along the main path which winds between mounds of quarry waste. In 100 yards you come to a junction of many paths where there is a short concrete route marker for a numbered walk — this spot is No. 6. To the right a grass path bears left through the bushes. If you go along here you come to the top of a tramroad incline which took stone down from Brown Stone Quarry. The two rows of stone blocks spaced at 3 ft intervals, which were used before sleepers, are slowly being covered by soil and grass. Return to the concrete route marker and go out to a clearing. Turn right and continue as before between and over the soil tips, past an OS pillar to go across a much damaged Iron Age camp.

Ahead is a topograph and a magnificent view. In 100 yards go through some bushes and turn right down into an old quarry to see the Devil's Chimney from close range. It is understood that the Devil has lately repointed his chimney as it was in danger of falling down. Sometime about 1800 an incline and tramway were made here to take the rock from the quarry down to the road where it was put into carts. In making the tramway a wall of rock was left on the left and this was later removed, except for the last part — the Devil's Chimney. As it could be seen from Cheltenham it became a feature of the many guide books then being written to make popular the 'Spa'. This part of the hill ceased to be worked by 1830 and rock falls and grass gradually covered the evidence of past activities.

To return to the car, walk back out of the quarry and keep ahead along the path with the wall on the left. Go down the side of the quarry in which the car is parked and either take a short cut down over the soil heaps or go out to the lane.

11

SHIPTON OLIFFE

WALK 2

★

5 miles (8 km)

OS Landranger 163, Pathfinder SP 01/11

The walk follows the old road, now a grass track, along the side of the valley to Withington and returns beside the little river Coln.

Shipton Oliffe is ½ mile north of the A40 Cheltenham to Witney road, 1 mile south of Andoversford. Take the lane, signposted 'Shipton', at the junction of the A436 with the A40. This lane goes through a group of houses forming Shipton Solers and on into Shipton Oliffe.

Cars can be parked along the wide road by the church in Shipton Oliffe. GR: SP 037 185. This church has two bells, the smaller church in Shipton Solers has only one. Shipton gets its name from Sheep-tun or farm. It is a village with two manors and in the 14th century one was held by 'Olyve' and the other by 'Solers'.

Leave the parish church on your left and walk down the lane to Shipton Solers. 100 yards beyond the sharp left-hand bend there are some very fine farm buildings on the left. Just beyond here is a small church set high above the road. It has interesting early wall paintings and a Jacobean pulpit — complete with hourglass — but as the church is nearly always locked the only way to see these is to go round the church and look through the window. The hourglass is within a yard of the clear glass of one window.

Continue to the main A40 road and cross to the A436 opposite. Go down this road for 200 yards and cross the grass verge on to the old road round the Frogmill Inn. Beyond the inn go over the old railway and just before reaching the main road again turn left along a good track. This track is the old road from Andoversford and the north to Withington. In ¼ mile it crosses a small stream, now by a bridge but originally by a ford which was, according to 14th century records 'The Foul Ford' — the name of the farm nearby is 'Fulford'. Soon the track crosses a long straight road, not Roman as it appears, but an enclosure road of the last century. It goes on past Thorndale Farm where it drops down to a gate and then along the side of the valley to Upcote Farm. The early settlers must have been influenced by the many springs which break out near the 600 ft contour, so they made their road a little higher up the side of the valley, even though it went far from the direct route.

On entering Upcote farmyard notice the large barn on the right, now the discreet hiding place for a modern grain silo. The doors were built to take the large wagons which were hauled into the centre of the barn to

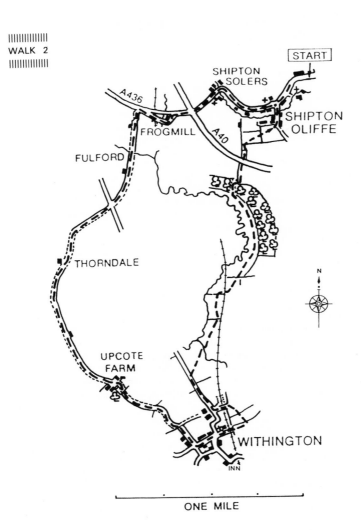

be unloaded. The large porch enabled a second wagon to be left in the dry should rain interrupt harvesting or in the evening for unloading next morning while the dew was drying in the fields. Across the yard, next to some pig sties, is a gate and the Old Road. From the high point in the third field there is a good view up the valley, now filled with many small fields. This was once one large field called 'Northfield', divided like an enormous allotment and farmed by the people of Withington. In 1819 an Act of Enclosure completely altered the way of farming which

13

had lasted for hundreds of years. The one large field was divided into farm units and this was followed by hedge planting and wall building, to give the pattern we see today.

The track continues down to a gate and then goes between hedges to a lane into Withington. At the road turn left past a row of much photographed cottages to the church.

Those wishing to visit the old Mill Inn should turn right downhill for 200 yards, returning to the church to continue the walk.

Below the church, next to the entrance to the Old Rectory, is a signposted footpath. Go down this path, passing under the bridges which connect the house on the left with the garden on the right, to a gate into a field beyond the railway bridge. Keep straight ahead near the hedge on the left for 200 yards to a stile on the left. Pass through this and go straight up the field to another stile. From here the path bears left to the top corner of the field where a gate leads on to a railway bridge. Looking over the right-hand side of the bridge you are looking at the old station, or rather, hidden in the mass of young trees, there is a platform — is it patiently waiting for just one more train? The station road ahead comes up to the road out of Withington.

Turn right along the road for ¼ mile to a stile just beyond a gate on the right. From the stile bear left across the marshy floor of the valley to a narrow plank bridge over a stream. This is the little river Coln which starts 4 miles away above Brockhampton and flows down to the Thames at Lechlade. Bear left from the footbridge to go between the meandering stream and a hedge on the right, into the corner of the field. Cross the fence and continue for ¼ mile with the disused railway on the right and the stream on the left. In the second field turn right under a railway bridge and then left towards the beginning of a wood on the hillside. On the left, a little beyond the next stile, is an excellent example of an 'oxbow', where the stream has scoured away the bank bypassing a large loop, which has started to dry up.

Continue up the valley, having on the right a wooded slope where Wych elms suddenly give way to oak, bordered by a hawthorn hedge mixed with maple, sloe, elder and willow.

Where the stream and valley turn left go straight ahead up to a gate and climb up the hillside between two woods. Before reaching the top bear right to go out of the wood and follow the boundary of the wood up to the left. Continue along the edge of the field to a gate onto the A40 road. Cross the road with care and go along a track opposite between hedges. In 50 yards go over a stile and follow the hedge on the left down to the corner of the field. Go across the next field diagonally to a gate and keep the same direction through another gate and so out on to a lane. Here turn left down to a ford and fork right on to the road through Shipton. The church and your car are 200 yards along to the right.

UPPER COBERLEY

WALK 3

★

5 miles (8 km)

OS Landranger 163, Pathfinder SO 81/91

This walk goes through the quiet Cotswold upland along unfrequented bridleways.

Upper Coberley is 2 miles from Cheltenham. It lies high on the wold ½ mile east of the road between Cheltenham and Cirencester and 3 miles west of Withington.

The walk starts at a road junction 300 yards above the handful of houses which make up the hamlet of Upper Coberley, where a gated road meets the road between Cowley and Withington. Cars can be parked on the wide grass verge at the beginning of the gated road. GR: SO 981 160.

Walk along the gated road for 200 yards and turn off to the right to follow the Cotswold Way sign and the bridleway sign which says 'Wistley Hill'. Keep to the track with the hedge on the left to the top of the field. Bear right and go into the next field to follow the hedge on the right. In 100 yards the track goes through bushes and trees for 50 yards. Just past the right-hand bend look across the field to the left as you will return this way from Wistley Hill. Keep to the track as it goes gently down between hedges and trees. This is another bridleway. A line of electricity pylons is unsightly in the countryside at the best of times but when there is a junction of four lines of gargantuan monsters the result is horrific. However, if you look at the wild flowers for the next few hundred yards you may not notice what is in the valley to your left.

Pass Needlehole, the house on the left, and cross the grass to join the drive. Follow this drive down the hill for ¾ mile and at the lane turn left up the hill. 100 yards up the hill look over a fence on the left, down into the dry flat floor of the valley. Continue up the hill and along the side of the valley to just past a blind left-hand bend. Here a track crosses. To the right it goes to a farm called Pegglesworth Hill. Here some Mercian land developer called Peccel had his 'worth' or enclosure. Turn left down the track with a wood on the left. Follow this track for over ½ mile to Pegglesworth Home Farm.

Turn right along the metalled drive and in ½ mile cross the main road with care. Five yards to the right a narrow footpath leaves the roadside. Go along this for 50 yards and after turning left and starting to descend the hillside bear left along an even smaller path which winds through the wood and gradually rises up to a hunting gate. Pass through the gate

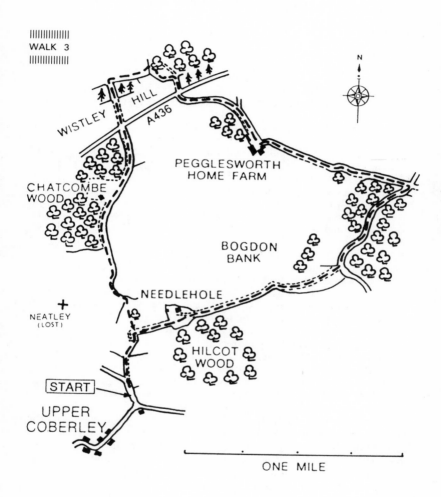

||||||||||||||
WALK 3
||||||||||||||

WISTLEY HILL

A436

PEGGLESWORTH
HOME FARM

CHATCOMBE
WOOD

BOGDON
BANK

NEEDLEHOLE

NEATLEY
(LOST)

HILCOT
WOOD

START

UPPER
COBERLEY

N

ONE MILE

and walk along the top of the escarpment. The fine view to the right is over the Dowdeswell Valley to Cheltenham. In 200 yards there is a gate on the left leading to a track through the conifer plantation. People walking the Cotswold Way have just toiled up the side of the hill from the reservoir far away below and arrive here in need of a few minutes' rest. Go through the gate and up the track to cross an open field to the main road. This is Wistley Hill, mentioned on the signpost at the beginning of the walk.

Again cross the road with care and keep ahead down to a gate. From this gate follow a track at the edge of Chatcombe Wood for ¾ mile. The gate at the other end of the wood looks down into 'Pylon Valley'.

Follow the edge of the field ahead, with the wall and bushes on the left. As the path swings round to the left, look over to the right, where 150 yards away there used to be a small settlement called Neatley. This comes from the Anglo-Saxon for a 'wet clearing', so there must have been plenty of water here once. Over the last 1000 years the level of water inside the hill has been gradually falling. Early settlers tended to set up house near springs — the Romans just below because they liked running water, and the following invaders above on drier land. When the water ceased to flow they had to move to lower land. Continue to the bridlegate in the corner of the field. From here the path crosses the next field to the trees and bushes on the other side, where the track started to go down to Needlehole at the beginning of the walk. Aim to pass to the right of a small clump of trees in the middle of the field.

When you reach the bridleway go to the right and retrace your steps along the side of the field, through a gate and down the next field to the gated road. Turn left to go back to the car.

COWLEY – COBERLEY

WALK 4

★

6 miles (9.5 km)

OS Landranger 163, Pathfinder SO 81/91

Cowley is 5 miles south of Cheltenham, just off the road to Cirencester.

The walk starts at the western end of a fine avenue of lime trees standing high on a hill bordering a lane 1 mile west of Cowley. From the A435 go straight through the village. From the A417 turn along a lane 1 mile east of Birdlip. This lane is not signposted but has small notices saying 'Stockwell', which is the name of a large farm half way to the avenue of trees.

Cars can be parked on the wide grass verge under the avenue of trees. GR: SO 950 146.

Walk along the lane towards the large farm called Stockwell and the A417, away from Cowley. Follow the lane round a sharp left-hand bend and notice the valley down to the right. You will come back up here. 200 yards past the corner, turn left into a field and with first a hedge and then a wall on the left go through two fields. Continue into the third field and go forward with the boundary, part wall and part hedge, on the right to a lane. Turn left along the lane up the hill. In 300 yards it is strange to see the hedge on the left cutting off such an odd-shaped piece of land. Did the road once pass along the other side of the hedge?

Continue down the lane until a narrow meadow appears on the right. Enter the meadow in the top corner by going over a wooden fence on the right. Keep to the edge of the meadow next to Cowley Wood on the right. As you go down you will notice that in the middle of the field there is evidence that there was once a stream here and it must have started near a bush in the middle of the field. At the end of the meadow go through a gate into a wood. In 50 yards the path turns right across what was once the dam of the (now dry) lake on the right. Turn left on the other side and go down the valley for ¼ mile to a gate. Beyond the gate follow the old track ahead and round to a gate and so on to a lane at the foot of Bubb's Hill. Turn left and go down the lane for 50 yards to the Green Dragon at Cockleford.

Opposite the Green Dragon a lane goes past the Girl Guide camping site. Go along this lane and after ¼ mile there is a fine view of Cowley Manor. Built in the late 17th century it has nothing in particular which makes it a 'Cotswold' building; it could be anywhere in the country. Follow the road round to the right and at the T-junction, turn right. The road now bends left past the entrance to the manor house and the

18

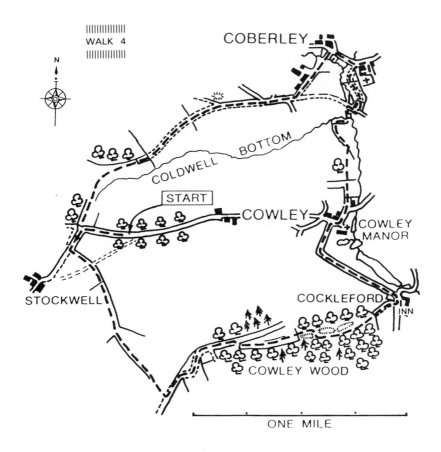

WALK 4

N

COBERLEY

COLDWELL BOTTOM

START

COWLEY

COWLEY MANOR

STOCKWELL

COCKLEFORD

INN

COWLEY WOOD

ONE MILE

church. To visit the church first read the small notice on the elaborate gates. Continue along the road and in 100 yards at the entrance to the 'Camp and Adventure Centre' on the left, when the road bears right, keep straight ahead with a high wall on the left. In a further 100 yards go over a stile and where the wall on the left ends keep the same direction over a fence and across a field. Pass about 20 yards to the right of a clump of trees. About 200 yards beyond the clump of trees there is a gap in the hedge which makes the right-hand boundary of the field. Go through the gap and turn left.

Near the corner of the field pass through a wicket gate into a new plantation. The Public Right of Way goes to the hedge in front and turns right to the corner where a path goes down to a footbridge over a stream. In the field beyond, walk up the bank and in 50 yards keep close to the wire fence on the right and go to a gate. Just past the gate is a grass lane. Turn right and go down this lane past a millpond on the left. Here is an old cloth mill; we know this because 18s tithe was paid on it in 1785. It has lately become a private house. Continue round to the right of the house and turn left across the front to a large gate into a field at the far end of the house. In the field follow the grass track until it comes out on the road near Coberley Court.

It is interesting to follow the signpost and walk up to the church. To do this go through the archway and in 30 yards enter the churchyard. A few yards past the gate look over the wall on the left at the end of a barn. The large beam once spanned the wide opening which was subsequently partly blocked up, needing a smaller beam over the opening. At a later date this too was reduced. Walk on round the church and almost opposite the porch there is a railed-off gap in the high wall, from here it is possible to see the old orchard beyond. It was here that the medieval Coberley Court once stood. Here, in the 14th century, lived Sir Thomas de Berkeley and his wife Lady Joan. When Sir Thomas died, Lady Joan married Sir William Whittington who died a few years after their third son Richard was born at Pauntley near Newent. It is said that Richard spent much of his childhood here, before being sent to London to learn how to deal in textiles and silks. He was, of course, the famous Dick Whittington who later became Lord Mayor.

Pass through the arch back to the road and turn left to the village of Coberley which is ¼ mile away from the church. On reaching the village bear left and in 20 yards turn left down a narrow path between a hedge and a fence. At the bottom of the slope cross the river Churn (a tributary of the Thames). Ignore the waymarking sign which indicates that a path goes to the left in the next field and keep straight ahead up the bank. Continue to the right-hand corner of the field and go through a gate. Go along the edge of the field on the left past the end of the stone barn and keep ahead to a cross-track. Turn right along the track and at the lane keep straight ahead. In 200 yards (10yards past a junction) the lane bears right. Here keep straight ahead through a gate. Follow the track along the side of the valley which is called Coldwell Bottom. When the track forks in ¼ mile bear left and gradually go down along the side of the valley.

In a further ½ mile keep ahead over two stiles and go on in the valley for 200 yards. Here the valley branches ahead and left. Bear left and follow the trees which mark the bed of a stream. There may not be any water flowing on the surface — it depends on the amount of rain that has fallen in the past few months. Go on up this valley past the spring to the road. Turn left to the avenue of lime trees and the car.

NORTHLEACH

WALK 5

★

5½ miles (9 km)

OS Landranger 163, Pathfinder SP 01/11

This walk goes over the upland around Northleach. In 1227 the Abbot of Gloucester granted Northleach a market, thereby elevating it to the status of a town. By the 14th century it had grown to be the principal wool-market of the central Cotswolds. In late Tudor times its wealthy wool merchants were spending their money on fine houses, as their fathers had done on the magnificent church. Ruled by the guilds, with their closed shop and inward-looking laws, Northleach was unable to adapt to the new methods of production and therefore does not figure largely in the 18th century picture. Consequently the industrial revolution, which so changed the Stroud valleys, had no impact on the town. It has remained almost untouched by the last two centuries.

Northleach is on the A40 road, 6 miles from Cheltenham and 5 miles from Burford. It lies just off the Fosse Way mid-way between Stow-on-the-Wold and Cirencester.

The walk starts 1½ miles west of Northleach on the old main road through Northleach towards Cheltenham. There is a wide lay-by 1¼ miles from the beginning of the new bypass, where the road to Bibury leaves the old main road. GR: SP 088 151.

On the opposite side of the main road there are two farm gates in the wall. Go to the one on the right and then down the edge of the long field beyond, keeping the wall on the left. At the bottom of the field there is a stile and a view down into a small dry valley. In the bottom of the valley there is a track. Go down to it and turn right. Follow the track for ½ mile to Hampnett. On reaching the lane turn right and in 30 yards bear left along a track which has first a wall and then a fence on the left, for ¾ mile to the Fosse Way near the bypass roundabout.

Cross the road and go down a good stony track between hedges. This is a part of the 'Northleach bypass' of coaching days. The fast through-coaches found the low lying main street through Northleach took too long so they came along this higher ground. In 200 yards the good surface turns right to Folly Barn but keep straight ahead for a further 100 yards. Now look carefully to the right for a stone stile. If you find a gate you have gone 5 yards past it. Go into the field and keep to the edge of the field with the wall on the right as far as a fence. From here the well-trodden path goes down the next field and then to the right of a row of trees where there used to be a hedge.

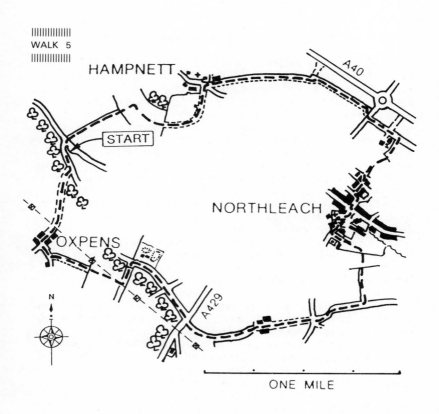

||||||||||||||
WALK 5
||||||||||||||

HAMPNETT

A40

START

NORTHLEACH

OXPENS

A429

N

ONE MILE

At the bottom go through a gate and bear left to a stile. Follow the path beyond to a second stile. From here go to the garden path and out on to the road. Turn left and in 10 yards turn right. In 50 yards go along a concrete path between gardens. At the end of the path turn left to the end of a wide metalled footpath. This leads to the main road in the centre of Northleach.

To continue the walk go to the top corner of the main square and through the churchyard. This great 'wool' church of the 15th century is worthy of examination. Leave the churchyard by the far corner to go down and in a few yards turn right on a narrow track between houses. At the road turn right and in 100 yards left in to the sports field. Across the playing field to the right is a tall bank with a stile in the centre which can be seen on the skyline. Climb the bank and stile and go straight up the field to another stile. Follow the path up the side of the field to a hedged cross-track. This is called Helen's Ditch and is another long abandoned bypass following the high ground.

Turn right along the track and at the road cross straight over onto a farm road. Walk on past the farm buildings on the right and then bear left on to a wide track between walls. At the end of the track go into the field and follow the wall on the right to a bridlegate and the main road. This is part of the Fosse Way.

Cross the road with care and go along the lane opposite for a little over ¼ mile. The planting of trees to improve the landscape began after the dissolution of the monasteries and reached its peak about 1850, aided in some cases by the Enclosure Acts. The owners of great estates planted narrow belts of trees on the edge of their land and the trees on the left are typical of this. Just past the grassed-over water tanks on the right, turn left through the trees on a wide grass track with a wall on both sides. In nearly 200 yards turn right through a gateway and go straight across the middle of the field to a gate.

Continue on the track through the next field and go down to a lane serving some cottages on the left. Turn right along the lane to Oxpens. When the lane turns sharp left, keep straight ahead for 10 yards and then turn right up the hill along a good metalled farm lane. Go through the belt of trees again on to the lane and turn left. In 300 yards you reach the main road where the walk started.

YANWORTH

WALK 6

★

5½ miles (9 km)

OS Landranger 163, Pathfinder SP 01/11

High on the hill looking across the valley to Stowell Park, Yanworth is on a lane 1 mile west of Northleach and 1½ miles east of Withington. The village is divided into two definite parts. To the east, the church and farm house with its fine collection of outbuildings; to the west, a handful of houses strung along a lane with a large farm in the middle. Cars can be parked along this lane near the village hall opposite which, in the wall, is the village pump. GR: SP 075 137.

Walk away from the telephone box towards the sharp bend at the east end of the village street. Turn left and in 20 yards turn right. This lane goes down to the church and farm. The church is mostly Norman and is well worth a visit. Those with keen eyes may well be able to find a number of scratch dials on the outside — the best one is just to the left of the porch one foot from the corner and about eye level. The farm buildings are very fine examples of the Cotswold style. Go on along the lane between two buildings, turn sharp right and down the lane for 200 yards, to turn left at the T-junction. As you go down the hill you will see, almost in front across the valley, the 17th century house of one of the great woolstaplers, James of Northleach. The Norman church behind the house is all that remains of the lost village of Stowell. Continue down the hill to the left-hand bend at the bottom and turn right through a field gate. Follow the wall with bushes through three fields to a lane. Opposite is an old mill and on the left the roadway is carried across the flat bottom of the valley by a causeway in which arches have been put so that the floodwater may escape.

On the opposite side of the valley go up a grass bank to a stile in the hedge on the left of the building in front. Later on, the walk returns through the gate on the right. From the stile go up into the wood following the trodden path, first as it bears left and then ahead down into a small valley. Follow the centre path straight up this valley.

When the wood ends, bear left up the field with the wood on the left. At the top, when the edge of the wood goes off to the left, turn right to go between two trees set in a vast field — which used to be eight smaller ones. Keep this direction up the field. If the path has not been reinstated look back from time to time to line up the two trees with the end of the wood. Eventually, when a wall comes into view, aim for a point 200 yards to the left of the wood where there is a wide stone step-over stile. Notice,

24

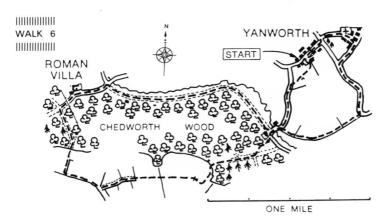

next to the stile, the end of the wall you would have been following years ago.

Keep the same direction across the next field and go to a gate and then follow the track to a grass cross-track. Go forward to the wall in front and look down into Chedworth Valley. Here houses, built on the spring line, perch at odd angles and streets twist and turn in unexpected complexity. The neighbouring villages of Colesbourne, Withington and Compton Abdale with Chedworth form a cluster of parishes each with names derived from the Anglo-Saxon and each having a Roman villa. In this isolated part of the Cotswolds the end of the Romano-British estate based on the villa may have merged into the Anglo-Saxon estate based on the village, and the parish boundary of today may have been the estate boundary 1700 years ago.

Turn right along the wall and follow the path around the edge of the field across the head of the valley. Go through a hunting gate and turn right, with a wall on the right. Keep the same direction over three stiles to enter a wood and in 50 yards bear left over a stile. Now follow this track ahead for just over ¼ mile to a sunken cross-track and a signpost 'Roman Villa'. Turn right and 100 yards beyond the railway bridge the track leads into the car park. The Chedworth villa is one of the finest examples of a Roman farm unit in England. It is well worth examining and the guide book is most helpful.

To continue the walk go down the lane to the Withington–Yanworth road. At the corner turn right through a gate on to a wide track with a wood on the right. 300 yards past the gamekeeper's cottage the undulations in the wood on the right, just above the track, mark the site of a Roman temple. At the end of the track go out onto the road and turn left. For the next 100 yards you are retracing steps taken on the way out. Go past the mill on the left and continue up the lane. In ¼ mile, when some of the houses of Yanworth can be seen across a field, turn right through a gate and go diagonally across this field up to a gate at the end of an avenue of trees. Walk up this avenue into the centre of Yanworth.

25

COOPER'S HILL

WALK 7

★

5 miles (8 km)

OS Landranger, 162, 163, Pathfinder SO 81/91

This walk is almost entirely through woodland, much of which is National Nature Reserve administered by the Gloucestershire County Council.

Cooper's Hill Picnic Area, View Point and Nature Trail are next to the A46, Cheltenham–Stroud road as it nears the top of the Cotswold escarpment. The picnic area looks down on a series of bends in the road which makes up what is known locally as 'Fiddler's Elbow'.

There are two signposted car parks which are connected by a fenced walk. The top one contains a toilet block and the walk starts from here. GR: SO 884 139.

Before starting the walk, it is a good idea to examine the notice board giving general information about the nature reserve, though there are more detailed notices at strategic places along the trail explaining what can be seen.

Start walking up the steps which lead round behind the toilet block and follow the blue arrows on the short posts. The colour of the arrow will change as the countryside changes. After climbing steeply for a short while, turn left along a well-used path. This is part of the Cotswold Way — Chipping Campden 32½ miles, Bath 57½ miles. When the track starts to go downhill bear right on to a narrow path. In 200 yards follow the Cotswold Way arrows to a hedged track between fields. In a few yards, when the track enters another wood, turn left. You will come back to this point near the end of the walk. Continue up the hill and after 200 yards the arrows are black. This route will take you to the top of the hill where you will see a very tall pole topped by a cockerel.

This is the site of the Cooper's Hill Cheese-Rolling Ceremony now taking place on Spring Bank Holiday, but long ago held at Midsummer. A 7lb Double Gloucester cheese is set off from the top of the slope with the competitors in hot pursuit. As the slope is 200 yards long with a gradient of 1 in 1, the St John Ambulance Brigade have to attend to many sprained ankles and bloody noses in what must be one of England's most dangerous sports. The ceremony is known to date back more than 1300 years and is similar to the pre-Christian festivities at Uffington White Horse and Cerne Giant. The cheese-rolling used to be followed by a scattering of sweets for the children and maypole dancing, both of which had their origins in fertility rites.

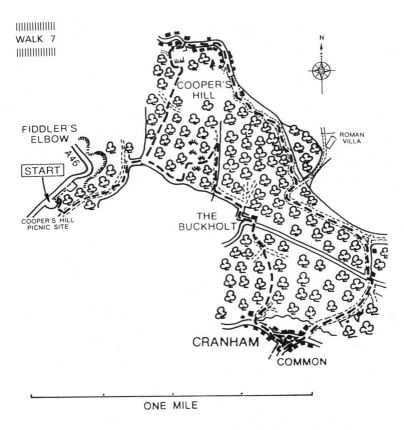

FIDDLER'S
ELBOW

COOPER'S
HILL

ROMAN
VILLA

START

A46

COOPER'S HILL
PICNIC SITE

THE
BUCKHOLT

CRANHAM

COMMON

N

ONE MILE

It is not advisable to imitate the local athletes in order to reach the bottom of the hill, so go to the left, following the yellow arrows marking the Cotswold Way. If you keep well to the left the path is not quite so steep. Go past the bottom of the hill and turn left on to a lane. Now turn right along the lane for ¼ mile. At the end of the lane go through a gate into the wood and follow the track with the wall on the left.

In ½ mile the track sweeps round to the right and another track goes down to the left. 200 yards down this track is the site of a Roman villa which has been laid out for visitors to walk round. Continue the walk on the original track for another ½ mile. When fields can be seen through gaps in the trees on the left, bear right at a fork, leaving the Cotswold Way to go on along the bottom of the wood. In a few yards a cottage can just be seen high up on the left almost hidden in the trees. As the track continues to climb, it improves and arrives at a road. Here turn left along the road and in 50 yards turn right on a metalled track through Cranham Wood. Follow the track down to a house and take the path to

27

the right of the garden. Continue along this path into Cranham. Cross the road and go up to Cranham Common, from which there are fine views down the Painswick Valley.

Below the last house on the right as you enter the main part of the common, there is a private car park belonging to the Black Horse. Go down here and opposite the Black Horse take the lane down to the lowest part of the village. Thirty yards past the village shop, near the bridge over a tiny stream, turn right into the entrance to the Scout headquarters. Pass the buildings which are on the left and go up the track into Buckholt Wood. In 50 yards bear left just before the track sweeps up to the right to a fork and follow the well-trodden path up the valley, twisting between the trees but keeping the same general direction and gradually getting steeper. As you go up, a track comes in from the left and you walk along it for a few yards. When it turns off to the right bear left up a narrow path. This path rises steeply to a gap in the wall. Take care here. One yard further and you are on the road. Cross to the safety of the grass verge on the other side and turn left.

Pass the house on the right and at the end of the garden hedge turn right off the road. The house is called 'The Buckholt', a name going back to the 11th century 'boc-holt' or beechwood. In 10 yards bear left along a track. After 50 yards follow the track to the right to go between gate posts into the estate of Witcombe Park. Turn left up a track just inside the wood, with the wall on the left. After 200 yards, at the top of the rise, go through a wide gap in an old crumbling wall and turn right.

This is an interesting old wood. It retains the character of an undisturbed Cotswold beech wood, unlike its neighbour Ebworth Wood on the other side of Cranham, where the old trees were cut down during the First World War to make rifle butts.

Continue through the wood with the wall on the right for 200 yards. Now look for a narrow path going back to the left. Follow this path across a clearing and into the wood again. In a few yards turn left over a stile and walk along the top of the ridge to the cross-track at the edge of the wood. Turn right and go down to the track between hedges where you came up on the way out.

At the other end of the hedged track turn left and retrace the route to the start of the walk.

ELKSTONE

★

2½ miles (4 km)

OS Landranger 163, Pathfinder SO 81/91

This attractive village is set high on the hills 3 miles south of Cheltenham and 4 miles north-west of Cirencester. It lies between two main highways out of Cirencester — the A417 to Gloucester and the A435 to Cheltenham. It is signposted at the Masons Arms on the A417 and is reached by going through Cockleford from the A435. Cars can be parked near the entrance to the church drive on the wide road which bypasses the village. Keep well clear of the church entrance and post box in the wall. There is plenty of room along the road. GR: SO 966 123.

Elkstone got its name from the Saxon Ealac. The exact stone is uncertain but some think it is the smaller one in the church vestry. The importance of stones can be traced back to prehistoric times and though Ealac was Saxon the stone is perhaps three times as old.

Here the church and large farm lie slightly apart from the main settlement. This part of the Cotswolds is full of interesting churches with much Saxon and Norman craftsmanship and Elkstone is the finest of them all. It is therefore fitting to make an exception to my usual practice of leaving churches to the many excellent guide books and briefly describe what can be seen, so that 'to be forewarned is to be forearmed'.

Those not wishing to visit the church should go down the church drive to the entrance to the churchyard and miss the next two paragraphs. Those wishing to see the church should turn right into the churchyard.

In front is the tower at the west end of the church. The large west window has a niche for the figure of the Virgin and Child and the west door has what is thought to be an Egyptian symbol of eternal life carved on the right. Stand near this door and look up to the top of the tower and see two of the four gargoyles — what a pity there is a modern downpipe to take the rainwater, for they must have looked marvellous spewing water in a storm. Round the corner there are two 17th century 'table' tombs and the south porch. Stand just inside and notice the lintels of the two small windows; these are 11th century grave corners. Over the south door is a fine sculpture showing Our Lord holding the Book of Judgement and giving the Blessing. The surround is one of the most interesting examples of beakhead ornamentation and here the birds' beaks hold the arch in position. But notice the odd one near the bottom of the left. Turn the ornamented door-ring and go inside the church.

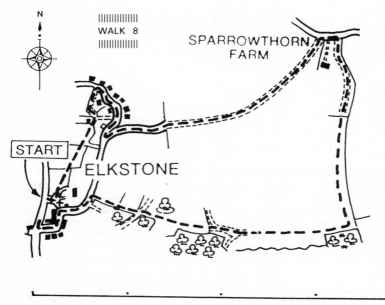

ONE MILE

There is an excellent and inexpensive booklet on sale which amplifies the information given here.

Go to the back of the church and look up at the roof of the tower which has some very fine carving. Low down on either side of the great arch are the remains of the wall-seating which used to go along both sides of the nave as it did in most churches — and gave rise to the saying 'the weakest to the wall'. On turning round and looking up the church to the east end the full beauty of the 12th century arches can be seen. Walk slowly towards the chancel arch and notice the interplay of the two arches and the lighting beyond. Carefully examine everything in the chancel — the bosses in the roof, the zig-zag moulding, the ornamentation round the small east window, the 17th century wood of the altar rails. . . . Before leaving the church go to the small door behind the pillar next to the pulpit; this reveals a narrow flight of stairs. Go up these to the 'columbarium' — this is most unusual but you will see what it is when you get there. To start the walk go back out of the churchyard to the drive.

Opposite the entrance to the churchyard a branch of the drive goes to what was once a coach-house. Go along this for 10 yards and turn left through a gate into a field and turn right next to the fence, past trees and bushes and then across the field to a stone stile in the wall in front, just to the left of a small clump of trees. Continue in the next two fields with a wall on the right to the far corner where a wooden stile leads on to a short grass path next to a garden hedge on the left. Cross the drive in front and go on between stone walls to a stone stile.

30

In a further 30 yards go over a second stone stile into the garden of Elkstone Court. The footpath goes round the left-hand edge of the garden to a metal gate and on to the road at the north end of the village. Turn right and walk along the road through the village. Just past the village school on the left the road goes downhill and turns right and then left past the springs which must have supplied water to the village in days gone by. Below here a rough lane leads back to the left between high banks. Go up this lane which soon becomes a farm track, especially after the gate at the top of the slope. It is in fact a council road. Continue for ½ mile to a road and turn right.

Pass the entrance to Sparrowthorn and in 50 yards turn right through a gate and follow the track down the hill. On reaching the valley bottom turn right along a cross-track with a damp hollow and poplar trees on the left. This track gradually climbs up the side of the valley for ¼ mile and then goes to the right of a wood to a gate ahead. From here go forward keeping about 20 yards to the right of the wood. At the end of the wood aim a little to the right of the left-hand group of trees on the ridge in front.

Just beyond the ridge, cross straight over a farm track and go down into a field with a hedge and wood on the left. Cross over a farm bridge at the bottom of the field and then climb up to a gate and so on to the road. Turn left in 50 yards and follow the road round to the right. On the right, in the corner of the churchyard is the house which was occupied by the priest from the 14th to the mid 17th century. Follow the road round to the T-junction and turn right back to the car.

SYDE

WALK 9

6½ miles (10.5 km)

OS Landranger 163, Pathfinder SO 81/91

Much of this walk is in wooded valleys and one part goes through long disused meadowland surrounded by woods. It is one of those solitary places, far away from houses and domestic animals, which has been included in this walk because here Nature is again quietly conducting her own business, untroubled by man. In the morning after a heavy dew or after rain the tall grasses, the hemlock and the giant thistles splash their beads of moisture all over the unwary traveller.

Syde is a small hamlet, a mile to the west of the A417 road. The signposted turning is 3 miles from Birdlip and 7 from Cirencester. Approaching the church from the main road the lane turns sharp left. It is possible to park here but make sure not to obstruct the barn doors. GR: SO 949 108.

Go down the road to below the church and turn right through two farm gates and into a field. Keep to the grass track as far as the end of the wall on the right. Here water gushes out under the corner of the wall from an exceedingly foul pond hidden by trees. Bear right down the field to a farm gate. Past here follow the winding track across the stream to a gate. Continue up the valley and at the far end of the 'L' shaped meadow will be seen a hunting gate and narrow path between giant wild flowers. In a further few yards cross the stream by the footbridge.

The next meadow is full of wild flowers and, in summer, butterflies. Continue up the valley between trees to a gate and into a field with a stone track across it 50 yards in front. Turn left along this track to pass through a gate and in a further 100 yards rise slowly past a series of muddy lakes on the right. The track continues to rise, with a wood on the left, until it goes past the end of Brimpsfield Park. Go up the drive, through the gateway and along the lane.

From this lane there is a fine view of Brimpsfield church across the valley. To the right, down near the wood, are the circular earthworks of the first Norman castle, made of wood. A second castle of stone was built to the left of the church, the remains of which are in the trees. There is very little of the castle left standing but quite a lot of it can be recognised in the walls and houses of the village. Only during a very dry spell can the remains of the 12th century priory be seen as parch-marks in the grass to the north of the church.

At the T-junction turn right into Brimpsfield village. In 200 yards

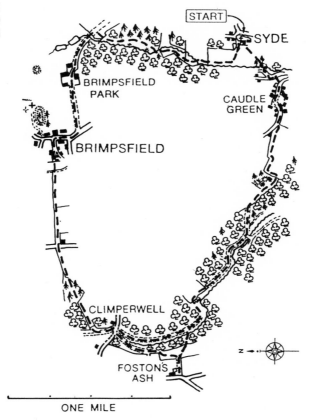

START

SYDE

BRIMPSFIELD
PARK

CAUDLE
GREEN

BRIMPSFIELD

CLIMPERWELL

FOSTONS
ASH

ONE MILE

turn left to the old centre of the village. After about 100 yards bear right and go along a narrow tarred pathway. From the stile at the end of the pathway go straight across the field and then a cross-track, to continue in the next field with the hedge on the right. At the end of the second field a track goes between two hedges to the lane at Longdale Barn. Cross the lane and continue with the hedge on the right. Go into the second field through a hunting gate in the corner and then into the narrow end of an old wood. Follow the track down and then go into the lower corner of a field. Now with the wood behind the hedge on the right go on down to the bottom of the field. Continue ahead, to bear left down into a valley and follow the edge of the wood round to a gate on to a lane. This is Climperwell.

On the other side of the lane there is a choice of two paths. Those who wish to make a slight detour to Fostons Ash Inn should take the right side of the valley and miss the next paragraph. Those who wish to continue the walk down the valley and back to the car should take the left-hand side.

Those bearing left should keep to the path close to the stream, ignoring any paths which go up to the left. In ½ mile a path comes down a narrow valley from the right. Now miss the next paragraph.

Fostons Ash is ½ mile away on the main road (B4070) between Birdlip and Stroud. From the road at Climperwell follow the track on the right which gradually climbs up the side of the valley, to go along just inside the wood until it suddenly turns right into the corner of a field. The path — a bridleway — now goes across the corner of the field to a gate in the hedge 200 yards away. Horse riders, who often use this route, have always gone round this field. It is no inconvenience to do likewise and follow the edge of the field round to the gate in the hedge. Turn right and follow the track to the car park of the inn. Return along the same track to the gate in the hedge. Now bear right across the field to the head of a small valley. Enter the wood and go down the narrow valley, cross the stream at the bottom and turn right.

Continue down the valley with the stream close by on the right. After 200 yards the path rises up to the left away from the stream and goes through a gate out of the wood. Turn right and go through a bridlegate leading to a pleasant winding track down the wooded valley. In ½ mile just past a small lake, keep straight ahead. In a further 200 yards bear left up through the wood. Go along the side of a field and through a narrow wood. Beyond the gate turn left up to the corner of the field and turn right to follow the wall on the left. Pass the barns and go down to a gate and so on to the road. Turn right down through Caudle Green. There was a notable spinning house here, 250 years ago, which employed many of the women and children of the area. Half way down the hill below the village, just past the garden of the last house on the left, go over a stone stile and straight down the hill to another stone stile, 10 yards to the right of a field gate.

Walk up the road opposite towards Brimpsfield. In 100 yards turn right down a house drive and go to the right of the house to a gate standing between two majestic Wellingtonia trees. Follow the track ahead up the side of the valley to the farm where the walk started.

PAINSWICK

The next two walks start from Painswick, which is called by many the 'Queen of the Cotswolds'. It is outstanding in an area known for its fine towns and villages. Some places have older houses, some have larger, none has whole streets whose intimacy and unity have been untouched by modernity.

The main road through the town takes most of the traffic so it is possible to walk leisurely round the streets and admire the domestic architecture of the past 400 years. The official guide to Painswick has much of interest about the people who have lived in and around the town. It costs only a few pennies and can be bought at the Little Fleece Bookshop in Bisley Street (which is well worth a visit in its own right) and at the post office. What follows is intended to supplement the guide book.

When compared to some towns on the Cotswolds, Painswick graduated late to adult life, only attaining 'market status' in 1321. By the 17th century it had a prosperous weaving community and became known throughout Europe for its coloured cloths. The clear soft water from the Midford sands, which overlay the upper lias clay, was ideal for dyeing. During the boom years of the 18th century there were a dozen mills, mainly fulling and gig, in the valley, and many looms in the town, especially in Vicarage and Tibbiwell Streets. By the end of the 18th century the smaller clothiers were in difficulty and the big new mills of the Stroud and Nailsworth valleys had gradually strangled the older methods of production. The clothiers of Painswick found it impossible to raise the capital to modernise and could not compete with the new mechanisation which the canal, and later the railway, helped to bring about by the cheap import of coal from South Wales.

Today Painswick is no longer a busy industrial town but its buildings are in good repair and it has an air of quiet prosperity. Its population in 1974 was 50 less than it was in 1801 and its sanitation is no doubt much improved.

Painswick is on the A46 road, 3 miles north of Stroud and 10 miles south of Cheltenham.

Cars can be parked in the large car park next to the main A46 road, 200 yards from the churchyard down the hill towards Stroud. Both walks start from here. GR: SO 865 095.

PAINSWICK – THE BEACON

WALK 10

★

4 miles (6 km)

OS Landranger 162, Pathfinder SO 80/90, 81/91

Walk up the main road past the churchyard to the traffic lights and turn left up the Gloucester road. Continue for nearly ½ mile until you are on the outskirts of the town. Just past the last house on the right turn right along a narrow lane. In a few yards bear left to walk next to the wall on the left. Continue round the bend to where the bushes on the right end, then bear right across the golf course towards the left-hand edge of a long wall. The old quarry workings and trees often make it difficult to see the golfers, so proceed with care. On reaching the wall keep to the lower right-hand track which goes across the first fairway and into the wood. In ¼ mile pass Catsbrain Quarry on the left. Continue along a track, cross a road and climb to Painswick Beacon and the hill fort.

The fort is known as Kimsbury Camp and is one of over 20 on the Cotswolds overlooking the Severn valley. It is roughly triangular in shape and has two entrances. One is near the summit where an ancient trackway comes up from Gloucester road. The other is near the middle of the opposite side. Much of the ramparts has been destroyed by quarrying but enough remains to give some idea of the work their construction involved. Each age had built in a different way from the ones which went before. No doubt this huge development astonished the local people just as the motorways do today.

Continue across the camp and down to the golf course on the other side. Bear right to a long straight track and go along it to a group of pine trees on the right. Leave the track and go down to the right of the trees to another track. Turn right and in just over ¼ mile, at a lane, turn left down the main road. Cross with care and turn right. This hamlet is called Paradise and it was a small weaving centre in the 18th century. Follow the road for 200 yards and just before the first house next to the road fork left down a lane signposted to Paradise. This house used to be an inn and, of course, it was called 'The Adam and Eve'.

The walk continues down the lane. Just past the garden wall of the second house on the left climb over a small stile in a gap in the wall on the left. Bear right down the valley and at the bottom of the first field cross the stream. It may be necessary to avoid the muddy patch by going a few yards to the left. Walk straight across the field to a gate into a wood.

A few yards inside the wood there is a stile on the right which takes you to another stile out of the wood. With your back to the stile, walk straight out into the field. The view across the valley is towards

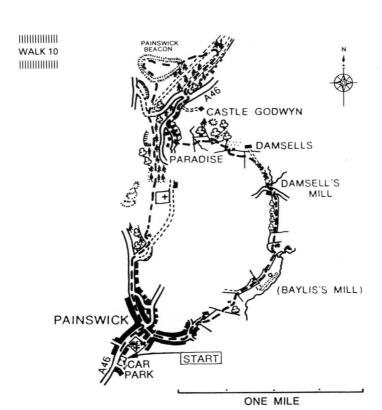

PAINSWICK
BEACON

CASTLE GODWYN

DAMSELLS

PARADISE

DAMSELL'S
MILL

(BAYLIS'S MILL)

PAINSWICK

CAR
PARK

START

N

ONE MILE

Painswick Lodge. It was here that Henry VIII stayed for one night when out hunting in the Coberley and Miserden woods. He had been unable to get back to Gloucester where he and Anne Boleyn were staying as part of a month's holiday in Gloucestershire after Anne's miscarriage.

Go down to a gate and into an orchard. Go ahead for a few yards and turn right down between the farm buildings to a stile and gate. In the field beyond turn left to a small gate, 20 yards to the right of the corner.

On the left is Damsells, a mill owner's house of the 18th century. Pass the remains of a very old tree and join the driveway. Walk along it to the road and turn left. This is Damsell's Mill. The mill pool was on the left at the junction of two streams. It is thought that originally there was a ford here. If you look at the bottom of the building you will see blocked-up windows which are now below road level. Continue past the old mill and turn right. In 5 yards bear left over a footbridge and go up to a stile which leads to a path through the wood. Continue as far as a T-junction and a wide farm bridge over the stream. From the many waymark signs choose the blue one to the right. This will take you along the bottom of the field to a gate.

37

In the next field the round building on the left was a wool drying tower. The embankment in the field behind the tower used to curve round across the stream, where there was a weir. The field away to the left and that part along behind the tower was the mill pool for Baylis's Upper Mill, which stood opposite the house now known as Highgrove. The mill was burnt down in 1830 and never rebuilt. Continue with a hedge on the right to a gate. Pass in front of Highgrove and walk along the lane. After crossing the cattle grid bear left over a stile into a field. At the other side of the field the way out is just out of sight round the hillside to the right of what looks like a small wood. Go to a farm gate with a stile alongside, and in the next field turn right up the hill to a stile in the top right corner, just above the large yellow house. Beyond the stile turn left.

On reaching the road keep ahead and go into Painswick. You enter the town up Vicarage Road and at the top bear left towards the church. The car park is 200 yards from the opposite corner of the churchyard.

PAINSWICK – JUNIPER HILL

WALK 11

★

4 miles (6 km)

OS Landranger 162, Pathfinder SO 80/90

Leave the lower end of the car park and turn left down Stamages Lane. Halfway down the hill go straight over the crossroads and down Stepping Stones Lane. Cross the bridge at the bottom. On the left is all that remains of Skinner's Mill, which is now a farm. In 50 yards, just past a house, turn right to follow the footpath sign along a lane. As you go along this lane you can look down across the field to the right to King's Mill House. The first record of a mill here was in 1495. Prior to 1820 it was a cloth mill but by 1858 it was for sale. The property then consisted of '. . . a building of three floors, a wool store, a drying store, a teasels house and other outbuildings . . . and two powerful water wheels.' The mill was still using water power at the beginning of this century. Most of the buildings have now been demolished and what remains is converted to a dwelling house. It still has the long weaver's windows on the second and third storeys.

Continue along the lane to Sheephouse. Just before reaching the house turn left and go past the front of the house. Look back at the gable-ends facing the courtyard where there are about 100 nesting-holes for doves. At the end of the wall on the right bear right to a metal V stile. This pattern is peculiar to the Painswick area and was probably the product of a local craftsman. Go up the path to another V stile and continue between trees — the remains of two hedges — to a gate. The path should continue between the two hedges ahead but these have become so overgrown that people have gone through the gate and have trodden a path along the edge of the field. In 300 yards go out on to a lane. Turn left and in 50 yards turn right up the lane to Bull's Cross. Walk up the lane for 20 yards and turn right on to a rough stone track. In 100 yards the track forks. Take the well-used track to the right and go up the side of the hill. Near the top there are fine views over the Painswick valley towards Pitchcombe.

Follow the track over the open top of the hill. When it starts to go down it meets the end of a lane. On the right is the farm track to Worgan's Farm. Turn left over a stile into a field with a small plantation on the left. The view to the right is over the Slad Valley. Walk along the edge of the field next to the wall on the left to a stile into a wood. Continue along the path which soon becomes a track. Most of the trees here seem to have ivy growing up their trunks. Follow the track for nearly ½ mile to where it starts to go down to a clearing.

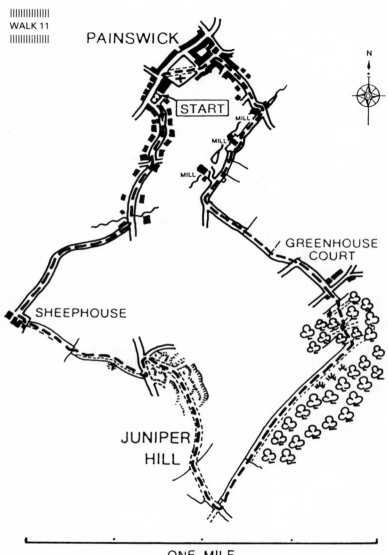

||||||||||||||
WALK 11
||||||||||||||

PAINSWICK

START

MILL

MILL

MILL

N

GREENHOUSE
COURT

SHEEPHOUSE

JUNIPER
HILL

ONE MILE

Behind the hedge on the left the field ends and another part of the wood starts. Turn left into the wood, having the boundary wall on the left. There are blue waymarking arrows on some of the trees here. (Blue = bridlepath, yellow = footpath.) Go down through the wood for 100 yards to a cross-track and turn left for a few yards, then back to the right and immediately left again down a narrow path. Cross another track and ahead down to a stile. This leads to a field with a wall on the right. As you go down the field look over the wall on the right to an unusual house which was, until recently, a most unusual barn. When viewed from Greenhouse Court the imposing castellated top of the barn was intended to elevate the mundane grain store into something much more romantic. Continue down the lane and cross with care because it is so narrow. Walk down the track opposite.

In 100 yards, when the track turns left to Dutchcombe Farm, go straight ahead into a field. Follow the hedge on the left down to a metal V stile and in the corner of the next field go over a wooden stile. The path now goes down the hill between hedges for 300 yards, where it is joined by a similar path coming in from the left. In a further 100 yards, when the track bears left down to what was once Mason's Mill, keep straight ahead, along a well-trodden path. In 50 yards go over a stile into a field and in a further 50 yards there is another stile, but here the path goes between hedges.

Continue to the right of the house ahead and across the lawn to the end of a lane. In 50 yards look down to the left; this used to be Cap Mill. As you go along the lane you approach another mill and can see the old weaver's windows on the top floor. This is Brookhouse Mill. It was converted to pin making during the last century and was making pins and paper clips 20 years ago. On reaching the road turn left. The dried-up mill pond is over on the right and the old building next to it was the dye-house at the time when the mill made cloth.

Walk on up the road and in 100 yards bear right into Painswick. This is Tibbiwell Lane and at the top, on the left, is Tibbiwell House. Opposite the old sign of the Golden Heart inn are two very attractive doorways. In the town the church is on the left and the car park is 200 yards down the main road from the opposite side of the churchyard.

RENDCOMB

WALK 12

★

2 miles (3 km)

OS Landranger 163, Pathfinder SP 00/10, 01/11

This walk is through typical open upland country. It starts on one side of a small valley and crosses through fields to go along a ridge overlooking Rendcomb. It returns across a grass valley. The village of Rendcomb was first mentioned in the Domesday Book as Rindecombe. Some people believe it means 'the valley through which the Hrinde stream flows' and that hrinde comes from hrindam, 'to push'. I think it may come from hrinde, 'the ring or bark', implying 'the valley of the barked or ringed trees'.

Rendcomb is ¼ mile east of the road between Cirencester and Cheltenham, and is 5 miles north of Cirencester. The walk starts from the post office and cars can be parked outside what was once the stable block belonging to Rendcomb Park. It is a very large building with a tall archway leading into a courtyard. It is now part of the school which is centred in Rendcomb Park. GR: SP 019 096.

Standing with your back to the stable block turn to the right and walk along the road through the village. Opposite the village hall, which is on the left, is the village pump. No doubt the news which is spread from here is more accurate than it was 100 years ago. 50 yards past the pump turn right through the garden gate of No. 12. Walk down the path at the side of the house and continue down the garden to a stile at the bottom. Go into the field beyond and turn left, keeping next to the hedge on the left. In 50 yards there is a fence with a stile near a big old tree. Past the tree the path goes along a ledge bordered by trees with a hedge on the left.

In 300 yards the hedge turns left and then continues along the valley. At this point look across the valley ahead to the other side of the field where you can see a path going up the hillside. Go down a grass track to the stream, step over the stepping stones and go up the path to a bridlegate in a few yards to the left of the corner of the field. In the next field turn right for about 20 yards and then bear left across the field towards the left-hand corner of the farmhouse overlooking the valley. There is a bridlegate here and beyond the gate a short steep rise to the end of a drive. The right of way goes up here and past the front of the house to follow the lane as it winds up the hill, passing the farm buildings on the left. Continue along the farm lane for ¼ mile to where it meets the road. Turn right on the road and immediately bear right

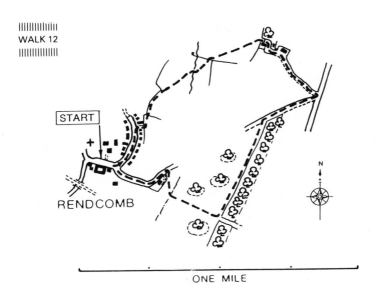

START

RENDCOMB

N

ONE MILE

along a lane which has a wall on the right and is open on the left. In ¼ mile, just past the end of a narrow wood on the left, turn left into the corner of a large grass field. Walk along the top of the field next to the wood on the left.

In nearly ½ mile there is a gate on the left leading to a track through the wood. A bridleway comes through here and goes straight down the hill to the right. Turn right and go down through a gap in the hedge — which has been neglected and become a row of hawthorn trees — and bear right. There is a hunting gate on to the lane just to the right of the entrance to what was once a small farm. (At the time of writing it is becoming a large house.)

On reaching the lane turn left and go up into Rendcomb. Turn left at the T-junction along the road and back to the start.

EDGE

WALK 13

★

5 miles (8 km)

OS Landranger 162, Pathfinder SO 80/90

Wooded hillsides and magnificent views can be enjoyed on this walk. Much of the route is on the Cotswold Way and is therefore well used.

Edge is a small village at the top of the escarpment 2½ miles south of Gloucester, on the A4173 road midway between Gloucester and Stroud. From near the church a road leaves the A4173 signposted Whiteshill and Randwick. ¼ mile along this road the rough land on the left is a common. In another ¼ mile a long quarry face runs parallel to the road. The walk starts at the footpath sign to Haresfield Beacon on the opposite side of the road to the quarry. GR: SO 845 092.

Cars can be parked at various places along the edge of the common.

Follow the footpath sign pointing into the wood. This is a part of the Cotswold Way and it says so on a small pointed white strip fixed to the footpath sign. Much of the walk will be on the Cotswold Way which is waymarked with blue or yellow arrows and a white spot. The path bears left and gradually goes down the side of the hill. On reaching a track go to the left. The wood above the track is National Trust property.

In ¼ mile there is an interesting house across the field to the right. It has six sides and a tall pointed roof, out of which sticks a yellow chimney pot. Follow this path through the wood for a further ½ mile to a lane. Turn right down the hill for nearly ¼ mile to a sign on the left at the entrance to Cliffwell House. The 'well' in Cliffwell is in a small building on the left. The inscription on the inside back wall is:

> Whoe'r the Bucketfull upwindeth,
> Let him bless God who water findeth;
> Yet Water here but small availeth,
> Go seek that Well which never faileth.

Continue up the path for 300 yards to a left-hand bend. On the right is a stone commemorating the siege of Gloucester in 1643. It was on July 26 that Prince Rupert had taken Bristol, which left Gloucester as the last Parliamentary stronghold between the west of England and York. The King hoped to open up the river Severn to his supply barges so he surrounded Gloucester on August 5. But the town held out for a month until six regiments of London train-bands joined with Essex's army and marched to the rescue. On the approach of these 15,000 men Rupert

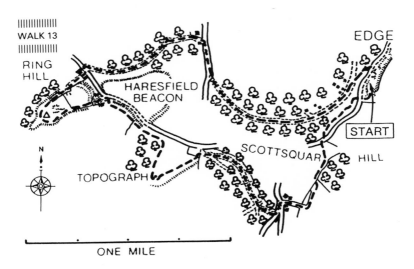

RING HILL

HARESFIELD BEACON

EDGE

START

SCOTTSQUAR HILL

TOPOGRAPH

N

ONE MILE

and the King withdrew. It is remembered as one of the few successes the Roundheads had in the first part of the Civil War.

Continue along the track to a lane opposite a farm. Turn left and in 20 yards turn right through a gate. Go up the slope and at the top bear left to go to the right of a gate. You have now entered the hill fort known as Ring Hill. Keep to the narrow path having a fence on the left and on to a stile. In the next field go ahead to the stone-faced Ordnance Survey column on Haresfield Beacon. Walk on round the fortifications with the valley on the right, to a V stile. Follow the path on to the lane near the National Trust sign. Turn down from the lane at the back of the enormous 'money-box' and bear left and with a wall on the left, go to a narrow gap in the wall which serves slim people as a stile. Others may go through the farm gate to the left! Follow the track up to the open land and bear right to a topograph. This shows clearly where the walk has been, starting from the wide grove above the last 'l' in Scottsquar Hill.

Set off towards London! In the far corner of the field go into the car park and turn right to go through a V stile in the wall. In the wood keep ahead and take the left fork along the track which forbids horseriding. In ¼ mile there is a bridlegate and 200 yards beyond, a junction of five paths. Here you leave the Cotswold Way which goes down to the right on its way to Bath, 49 miles away.

Bear left along a path which goes to the corner of the wood and out on to a lane. Turn left and in 200 yards, at a T-junction, turn left. Keep to the wide grass verge for 30 yards then cross the road to a house driveway. Go down a narrow track between walls to a gate into a field before turning left round the corner of a wire fence. Continue by the fence and then bushes to the corner of the field and go over a stone stile. Turn right along the bottom edge of a field for about 100 yards to where the wall on the right starts to curve round to the right. Here bear left up the field, going to the left of an electricity pole, to a V stile in the wall 30 yards to the left of a gate.

On the road beyond, turn right for 10 yards and then cross the road. Go into the wood along a narrow path. As you go down into the wood bear right parallel to the road. In ¼ mile this path curves round to the road opposite the end of the common where the car is parked. Cross the road and walk along the common to the car.

SLAD VALLEY

WALK 14

★

4½ miles (7 km)

OS Landranger 162, 163, Pathfinder SO 80/90

The Slad valley is well-wooded at its northern end where it is divided by a high tongue of land. The two valleys so formed are steep-sided and narrow. The walk is in remote wooded valleys and high uplands and passes isolated cottages which are still lived in.

The walk starts at Bulls Cross, which is high on the hill which separates the Painswick and Slad valleys. It is 1 mile south-east of Painswick, from which it is signposted but the lanes are very narrow. It is also reached by going 3 miles north from Stroud along the B4070 road towards Birdlip.

There are a number of parking places, the best being near the B4070 at the crossroads. The description of the walk starts from here. GR: SO 877 087.

Walk along the main road towards Birdlip for 100 yards to a footpath sign. Turn right and go down a track. Follow the track down and round to the right. After a short level stretch it curves down and round to the left. Now look for a narrow path which goes down to the right to cross the floor of the valley just below a dam. The lake has been made here to provide water in the event of a woodland fire. Continue up to the cross-track. Immediately ahead is a narrow and steep path up through the trees. Climb up to a track along the top of the ridge.

Turn left, uphill along the track for ¾ mile to a T-junction. For the last few yards of the track it might be more pleasant to keep one's eyes on any birds there are in the field on the right. At the junction turn right and pass the farm behind the wall on the right, to a rough track, having the wall on the left. Follow the track for ½ mile down into a wood. Continue following the main track down to Dillay. Keep to the track when it turns to the right between the house and a barn, and at the end of the garden wall turn left. In 10 yards turn right through a gateway to go down the steep side of an old orchard to a footbridge. After crossing the stream turn right and in 50 yards bear left up the hillside to where there is a stile. Go down and follow the path past the end of a cottage. In front of the cottage bear right up a wide grass track between walls and in 50 yards go through a gate on the right.

Walk along the bottom of the field next to the hedge on the right. In ¼ mile, at the second hedge, go over a stile which is halfway up to the wood on the left. The wood is a Nature Reserve administered by the

47

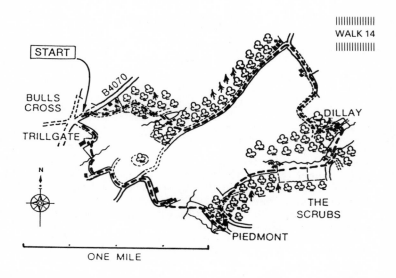

Gloucestershire Conservation Trust. The various county conservation trusts aim for '. . . the continued existence of the greatest variety of wildlife through the conservation of the widest possible variety of ecological habitats. . . .'

Walk along below the wood for nearly ¼ mile until you can see a stile in the fence on the left. From here bear right up to a track and turn right to go round the end of the wooded hill. Beyond the gate follow the wider track up to a house and the end of an asphalt road. Here bear right down a concrete road. At the bottom, at the entrance to a house, turn back to the right and walk through the garden to go just in front of the house. Continue past another house and follow the path along and then down to a small gate from which there is a view across the valley to a farm. In the field below the farm there is a clear path through the grass.

Go down to a small bridge and up the path to the left of the farm and on to the end of a metalled lane. This is the other end of the Nature Reserve. Walk up the lane and in 300 yards pass a house on the right with a well-head against the wall on the left. Continue up the lane to where a track joins from the right.

Go down the metalled lane for 100 yards and at the first left-hand bend turn right along a track. On the hill in front is Bulls Cross where the walk started. In 200 yards the track forks. Bear left, down towards a house. 50 yards from the house turn right through a gate and walk round the bottom of a field, with a fence on the left. Follow the edge of the field down to a stile on the left of a farm gate. Climb up the field in front towards the right-hand end of the buildings, where there is a stile. At the road turn right and walk up to the crossroads at Bulls Cross.

DUNTISBOURNE ABBOTS

WALK 15

★

6 miles (9.5 km)

OS Landranger 163, Pathfinder SO 80/90

This walk goes up to the village of Winstone, high on the hills, to cross a deep valley to Miserden and return across the valley and the high open land to the west of Duntisbourne Abbots.

Duntisbourne Abbots lies ¾ mile to the west of the main road between Cirencester and Gloucester A417, the Ermin Way. It is 5 miles from Cirencester. Approach the village from the A417 by the road which starts 200 yards south of the Five Mile House.

At the beginning of the village the road goes down past new houses into a narrow valley. You will walk back to this point and go up the valley to the right. Continue up the hill and at the top, turn right. Keep straight ahead for 200 yards to the second turning to the left and follow the sign 'unsuitable for motor vehicles'. Fork left immediately, and park on the left-hand grass verge at the beginning of a track. GR: SO 969 078.

There are four Duntisbournes. Starting from the south there is Duntisbourne Rouse which belonged to the 13th century Sir Roger de Rous; Middle Duntisbourne; Duntisbourne Leer which belonged to the Abbey of Lire in Normandy, and Duntisbourne Abbots which belonged to the Abbey of Gloucester.

Walk back through the village and turn left at the YHA house. Go down the hill to the footpath sign to Winstone on the left at the bottom and go into the meadow. Follow the valley for nearly ½ mile. The course of this dry valley, like so many others on the Cotswolds, was decided many thousands of years ago in the Ice Age. It was then the meander of a small river. Gradually the level of water stored in the cavities in the limestone has dropped and the first sign of a small stream is now some way down the valley.

There is a hunting gate in the corner of the field where a tall hedge crosses the valley. In 20 yards go through a second gate and cross a track to a third gate. In 50 yards go over a stone stile to the left of the fourth gate. Continue up the valley with first a wall and then a hedge on the left. Pass between two woods and at the end of the wood on the left keep straight ahead to a stone stile 5 yards to the right of the house in front. Winstone church is over to the right, separated by ½ mile from the village. At the lane bear left past the barn with the large arch and go into Winstone. At the village, fork left and in 200 yards join a road. 100 yards

49

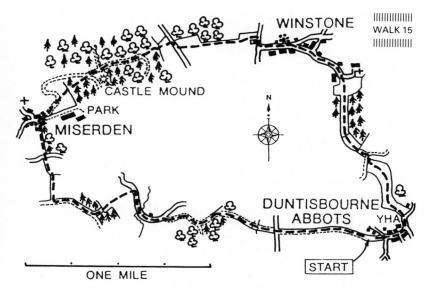

WINSTONE

CASTLE MOUND

PARK

MISERDEN

DUNTISBOURNE ABBOTS YHA

START

ONE MILE

past the last farm buildings on the left, where the road turns sharp left, turn right.

In a few yards, just past the modernised cottage, turn left at the first footpath sign. In the field, follow the wall on the left and when it ends, walk parallel to the hedge on the right. After 200 yards follow the hedge on the right. When the wood ends keep the same direction across the field to a stone stile in the hedge 10 yards to the left of an electricity pole. There is a footpath sign near the stile but it is difficult to see from the end of the wood.

In the lane turn right and in 50 yards turn left through a gate. With your back to the gate aim to the wall on the opposite side of the field; the footpath sign directs you too far to the right. There is a stone stile in the wall a few paces to the left of a small hunting gate. The path now goes down into a wood. First it passes to the right of a large beech tree and then curves down into the valley to a well-used metalled roadway. This is part of a network of service roads on the Miserden Park Estate. Follow the road down the hill to a stone bridge over the young river Frome. Look over the left-hand stone parapet and up between the trees to the Castle Mound.

Continue along the roadway for 150 yards and at the junction, bear left across the road to a track which goes up through the wood. Follow this to a stone stile and then go up the bank ahead to join the roadway again as it goes up to the gates, out of the park and into the village of Miserden. 200 yards past the gates there is a footpath sign on the left. This is the way back. Follow the sign along a path which goes at the back of a cottage. Go over a well-worn stile and across the field near to the wall on the left. Cross the lane and go through the gate opposite. Keep the wall on the right through the next two fields. At the cross-track turn left downhill and in 300 yards, where the track forks, bear left between hedges down to a gate. From here you can see a gate at the bottom of the field. Go down the field but when you get to the end of the hedge on the right, look at the view across the valley. Duntisbourne Abbots is over the hill to the right.

At the lane at the bottom of the field turn right and go down the hill. 100 yards past the house in the valley, at a left-hand bend in the road, go ahead to a gate. This is the start of a track over the hill. In the field bear left and go up the hill for 300 yards to a fork. Keep to the left along the hillside for 50 yards before going up between woods to two stone gateposts. Continue through the field with the fence on the right. This path gradually improves and becomes a track. At the crossroads go straight over. The car is ½ mile away at the other end of this track.

BIBURY – COLN ST ALDWYNS

WALK 16

★

5 miles (8 km)

OS Landranger 163, Pathfinder SP 00/10

This walk from Bibury winds it way along the bank of the river Coln to Coln St Aldwyns, returning over a small hill to the south.

Bibury parish is made up of two parts; Bibury itself to the east and Arlington to the west. They are divided by the river Coln. Much has been written about the beauties of Bibury and it would be interesting to know how many photographs there are of Arlington Row.

We know people have lived hereabouts for over 2000 years and perhaps much longer; in the camp above Arlington and the Roman building downstream from Bibury Court; through traces of Scandinavian and Norman French in the church, to Medieval, Tudor and Georgian domestic architecture. The best impressions are gained from walking round the two parts of the village away from the main road. Arlington Mill should be visited if possible and the inexpensive leaflet obtainable there is very helpful.

Bibury is on the A433, 6 miles from Cirencester and 9½ miles from Burford. It is well signposted.

Cars can be parked in the car park opposite the Trout Hatcheries. GR: SP 114 068.

Go along the well-used footpath opposite Arlington Mill. On the left is Rack Isle, a field now rather overgrown, where cloth was hung out to dry in the sun after fulling. At the end of the path turn left past the famous Arlington Row. A few yards past the last house follow the footpath sign to the right and go up a track at the back of Arlington Row. During modernisation which took place in 1975 the fronts remained unaltered whilst the backs were transformed and the old earth closets abandoned. (A cottage in the middle of the row had a fine two-holer.) At the top of the bank turn left in the field next to the wall along the top of a wood. After ¼ mile the path swings out a little way from the wall and goes through a gate, to descend the last field on a track. The large house in front was built a few years ago and though it looks 'Cotswold Traditional' it has all the modern building improvements.

Turn right along the road and at the top of the hill go along the left-hand track above the wood. Pass the turning on the right to New Barn and follow the wall on the left down into a small valley. From the gate into the meadow bear slightly left round the hill to another gate.

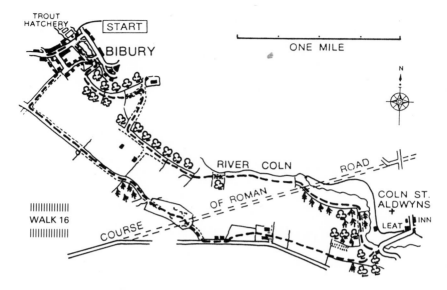

This leads to a fenced track for 200 yards, followed by a pleasant walk next to the river Coln for ½ mile.

On entering a long narrow meadow stretching away to the right, look straight ahead at the stone walls and sluice gate at the end of a wood. This is the beginning of a long man-made channel which is an alternative to a mill pond. It is called a leet and this one is nearly ¾ mile long, curving round the other side of the valley to the mill below the church. Arlington Mill has one of about the same length.

Turn right along the right-hand side of the meadow. In 150 yards you are crossing the line of an old Roman road. It came down the hill from the right, went across the floor of the valley and over the hills in the distance to the left of the houses in front. On the way back a short length will be seen in a field. Continue along the edge of the meadow and then follow the path through a wood. In the meadow beyond, keep ahead to a gate with a footpath sign pointing up to the right. That is the way back. Those wishing to go straight back should miss the next paragraph.

To go into Coln St Aldwyns walk on past the lodge, out to the road and turn left. In 300 yards, at the beginning of the village there is a sharp left-hand bend round what was once a flour mill. The New Inn is 100 yards up the road on the right. The return walk starts from the signpost in the field behind the lodge, so retrace your steps along the road.

Go up the field between an avenue of old trees and bear right at the top near the wood, to a gate. Follow the faint track ahead and after the next gate look down into the valley on the right, where there is a steep-sided trench some 300 yards long which gets smaller as it goes up the valley. It terminates suddenly at a wall, as if it once went on into the next field where it has been ploughed out and completely vanished. Continue with a wall on the left to a gate. The path goes straight across the next field to another gate. When the field is cultivated a strip is usually left unplanted so that the path is quite clear. Beyond the next gate go along a farm track opposite, with the cottage on the right, and when the track turns left to the farm buildings go straight ahead. In 100 yards go through a gate and across the field towards a house in the opposite corner. Just before the corner there is a gate in the hedge on the left. This tall gate is made with long vertical slats but can be opened easily by a rider on a horse. Go through to the road and turn right.

Walk along the road for 300 yards and at the end of the first field on the right turn right and follow the footpath sign. As you go down look over to the right at the stone wall. A few yards down from the right-hand end the wall appears to go over a flat shelf in the slope. This is where a Roman road starts to cross the field on the right. Go through a gate into a very uneven field. Follow the track down for another 50 yards until you can see a short grass track on the left. Turn back to the right and you will see a continuation of the track going up to a wall. It has been ploughed out in the surrounding fields. This is Akeman Street, part of the Roman road from Exeter through Cirencester to the Watling Street near St Albans. The standard Roman road was 84 ft wide with the centre 17 ft 3 in metalled with a camber. The verges were for horsemen and the edges marked with a ditch. On the other side of the field on the left it becomes a lane for 3½ miles. Away to the right short lengths can be recognised. There are 150 yards as a road north of Coln St Aldwyns; some tracks in the deer park at Hatherop; a lane over the hills near Eastleach and then it is sometimes a bridleway (Walk 20), sometimes a footpath.

Continue down the track and go up the other side of the valley next to a wood. At the top of a hill the track continues for ¾ mile. After ½ mile, at the end of the first field, there is a clump of bushes on the left of the track. This was probably a dew-pond, now much overgrown. When the track starts to descend it comes to a cross-track. To the right it is a grass strip, to the left a narrow track. Turn right for nearly ½ mile.

At the corner of the field turn left at the many-armed signpost and go down the side of a field. After passing the garden of the Catherine Wheel Inn cross the main road and turn right down to the mill at Arlington.

BIBURY – ABLINGTON

★

5 miles (8 km)

OS Landranger 163, Pathfinder SP 00/10

This second walk from Bibury goes mainly over the open hill to the north.

Leave the car park by the well-used footpath opposite Arlington Mill. The overgrown field on the left is Rack Isle where cloth was hung out to dry. At the end of the footpath step carefully between photographers and go past Arlington Row. This was once a 14th century wool warehouse. At the main road turn right and in 100 yards, where the main road bears left, keep straight ahead down a one-way street.

This is Old Bibury where every house is worth a second glance. Continue past Church House with the church behind and the long wall of a barn next to the entrance to the school. Walk up through the village to the main road. Almost opposite, across the main road, a lane goes up the hillside. It starts where the main road turns right. Go up this lane to the house at the top which overlooks the valley. Pass the house and continue ahead along a track. Soon Bibury Farm comes into view over to the right. In ½ mile descend to a gate into a large field and in a further 100 yards go past Hale Barn on the left. Keep near the wall on the left to a gate in the corner of the field and then out at a cross-track. Turn along the track to the left.

This is part of the Salt Way, where merchants from Droitwich came with their animals laden with salt — one of the few commodities the town and village communities could not produce themselves. In past ages there were few chemicals available so salt was used in most unlikely trades — for the preparation of clothing, the construction of buildings and even for the relief of toothache. But it was used chiefly in preserving food, from pork and cheese to herrings for the Catholic world. This Salt Way led to Lechlade which was the highest navigable place on the Thames.

Continue along this track for ¾ mile to Saltway Barn and when the track bears left to go on the opposite side of the hedge, turn left. Proceed across a short length of an old concrete runway to go along a track between fences. Follow this track for 1 mile over the hill and down into Ablington. At the road keep straight ahead down a narrow lane with an attractive cottage on the right. In 150 yards at the T-junction with a road, turn right. Go past the Manor House behind the wall on the left and follow the road round to the left until you reach the bridge over the

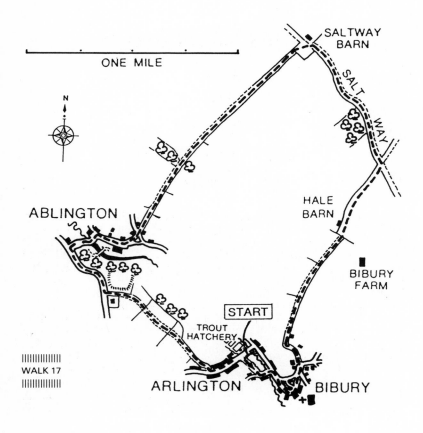

ONE MILE

N

SALTWAY BARN

SALT WAY

ABLINGTON

HALE BARN

BIBURY FARM

START

TROUT HATCHERY

||||||||||||
WALK 17
||||||||||||

ARLINGTON

BIBURY

river Coln. Look over the right-hand side of the bridge at the original route of the road. Until the end of the 17th century, bridges were rare. Here a narrow clapper-bridge would have sufficed for pedestrians and everything else went through the water.

Walk along the road and rise up to a T-junction. Turn left and go up the hill. There are some places along the bank on the left from which it is possible to look down at Ablington Manor in the valley below. At the top of the hill the road bears right. After a few yards turn left following a footpath sign into the drive of a house. Walk across the mown grass to the left-hand corner of the garden. From here follow the path through three fields to a track past a farm on the left. This is an outlying part of Arlington. Continue to the main road and turn left. At the bottom of this hill are the Trout Hatcheries and the car park.

EDGEWORTH

WALK 18

★

9 miles (15 km)

OS Landranger 163, Pathfinder SO 80/90

Edgeworth is a very small village looking down into the narrow wooded valley of the river Frome. It is 5 miles north-west of Cirencester and is reached from the B4070, Stroud to Birdlip road by going south from Miserden; from the A417 Cirencester to Birdlip road by going south-west through Duntisbourne Leer, or from the A419 Cirencester to Stroud road by going north through Sapperton.

Cars can be parked on the grass verge near the small bridge where the lane crosses the valley floor, ¼ mile north of the church. GR: SO 951 064. The approach from either side is steep and particular attention should be paid to keeping the lane clear.

Go up the lane towards Duntisbourne with the little river Frome and village of Edgeworth on the right. 200 yards from the bridge, as the lane curves gently up to the left, turn off to the right through a gate and down a track. This was once one of the drives to the Manor House, for at the bottom you will find a beautiful stone bridge. Notice how narrow it is and the recess for the lad who was holding the gate open. Was there only a ford here until the 18th century? This can be the only reason for the old stone footbridge just below the bridge. Continue up the old drive between an avenue of trees to pass below the Manor House. The drive then curves round to the right to go between stone pillars onto the road. Ebworth Manor stands on a site where people have lived for many centuries. Parts of the present house date back to the 17th century.

Facing away from the manor gates go along the road and in 50 yards fork left down a lane. In 200 yards the lane ends at a gate. Go through and follow the grass track round to the left. In a few yards it will be seen that the clear track goes on round the valley to a gate. Do not follow this but take the faint track ahead up the opposite side of the valley to a stile and gate at the top. Beyond this keep to the edge of the parkland, next to the fence on the left. Continue in the same direction, with a wall on the left in the next field, for ¼ mile. At the end of this field there is a cross-track. This place is known as Gloucester Beeches from the trees on the left. Turn left along this track and go down past the shell of Pinbury Cottages to a gate and into a rough wood. Turn to the left and go down an old track which soon curves round to the right and then on down to a small ford. Only in very wet weather is there much water here as the river Frome has gone underground. From the track beyond the ford it is

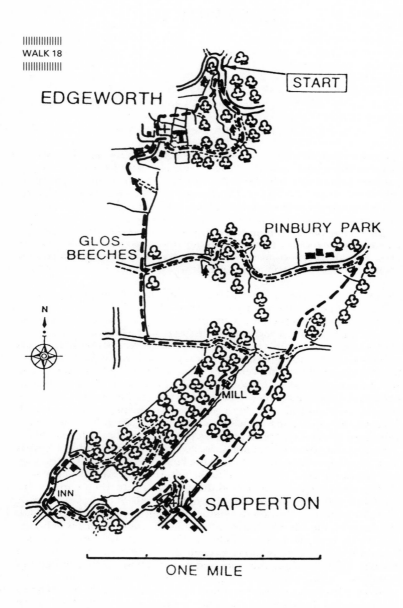

||||||||||||||
WALK 18
||||||||||||||

EDGEWORTH

START

PINBURY PARK

GLOS.
BEECHES

N

MILL

INN

SAPPERTON

ONE MILE

possible to look down into the almost dry bed of the river. Continue along the track to join the road past Pinbury Park.

Nearly 200 yards past the last building on the left and just past a small pond on the right, turn back to the right round the pond along a grass track to a farm gate. This bridleway goes along the side of the valley and does not vary in height more than 25 ft over the next 1¼ miles. After the gate the path rises slightly to pass to the right of a narrow wood.

Just past the next gate a good track comes down from the left and with some difficulty it can be seen to go down to the right. For about 300 years from the middle of the 15th century this was the road along which the prosperous merchants of the Bisley area used to send their cloth to Cirencester and then on to London. With the making of Cirencester Park the route was extended to go either through Daglingworth or further south along what is now the A419 and which was turned into a turnpike road in 1751. Cloth was wrapped in packs of ten and taken by packhorse or men, who spent their lives walking with 50 lb loads. On the way back you will follow the route as it climbs the other side of the valley. Because of the almost non-existence of roads in some areas of the country it was easier to send the cloth to London and from there to other parts of England. This was a good road at one time but, no doubt, there was plenty of broad Gloucestershire cursing as the heavy loads came up out of the valley.

Continue the walk almost in a straight line through gates and over stiles to the road at Sapperton.

The next part of the walk starts by going down a narrow pathway to the left of the churchyard and then turning right to go just below the church. Go on across an uneven field and down to a new fence. Here turn back to the left, rising slightly and after 100 yards cross the top of a long sloping meadow to a field gate, partly hidden behind a bank, halfway down the field. This leads to a track through the wood. In 20 yards look for a faint path on the right which doubles back and goes down to the western entrance of the canal tunnel. (For a little information about this 18th century canal and tunnel read Walk 22 which passes the eastern entrance 2 miles away.) On the left is the remains of the Watchman's House, built in 1792. 150 years ago this part of the canal would have been teeming with activity. Unlike later canal builders the Thames and Severn builders assumed that barges would be pulled by men, as they were on the Severn when the wind and tides were not favourable. They therefore allowed stiles instead of gates on the towpath and effectively prevented the use of horses, which were soon to replace men on the waterways of the rest of England. Follow the towpath for just over ¼ mile to a road where it goes over a bridge. The long building on the right started life in 1784 as Tunnellers Lodging but it afterwards became the Bricklayers Arms and it is now the Daneway Inn.

Go up the lane at the back of the inn signposted to Edgeworth. In 300 yards just past the entrance to Daneway House, bear right up a track which curves round to the right. In the wood keep to the right and go over the ridge. In a few yards fork right, pass a gate on the right and keep to the main track along the hillside for nearly ½ mile. At a cross-track, where a well-walked track goes down to the right, turn right and follow the track down and then round to the right again. On nearing the bottom of the valley look for a path turning back and down to the left. Turn left and follow this path along the bottom of the wood. In ½ mile you pass the ruins of Henwood Mill, one of the many small mills which used to fill this quiet valley with noise and activity. At the ford turn left. This is the route that the cloth merchants used to send their wares to Blackwell Hall in London.

Go up out of the wood and along the edge of a field. Where the track starts to go between hedges turn right through a bridlegate into the corner of a field. Continue with the wall on the right and keep ahead over the cross-track at Gloucester Beeches, to follow the outward route back into Edgeworth.

Arriving again at the church go into the churchyard and keep to the left along a path to a lych gate and a flight of steps leading into a field. From here the footpath bears right, following the line of four flimsy stiles in some new wire fences, to a farm gate which is down the hill just out of sight from the churchyard. Beyond the gate a track leads down and round to the right — do not follow this but bear slightly to the left of the track and go down a fairly steep bank.

At the fence turn right and go up the water meadow to a gate at the far end and the start of the walk.

BISLEY

WALK 19

★

4 miles (6.5 km)

OS Landranger 163, Pathfinder SO 80/90

This walk is through pleasant farmland and a well-wooded valley. Bisley stands high on the hills above the Stroud valley. It is 4 miles east of Stroud, 6 miles south of Birdlip and 2 miles north of Charlford. It is signposted on the A419 and B4070.

The houses of the village of Bisley huddle together at the very top of the Toadsmoor Valley and the narrow main street forms part of a large circle round the church.

Cars can be parked along the road at the front of the Bear Inn. GR: SO 902 059.

Before starting the walk, inspect the small building a few yards from the Bear inn, opposite the entrance to the school.

Here is a reminder, in the form of a twin lock-up, of the somewhat rough treatment meted out to those who were drunk, and when times were often very hard there were many of these. Go down the road away from the inn and on reaching the bottom, turn right down the main street. In 100 yards fork right and in another few yards right again. On the right are the Seven Springs with their elaborate stone piscina. On Ascension Day each year these springs are 'dressed' with flowers and blessed by the church though the custom has its origin in prehistoric times. Take the next turning to the left and then keep ahead. This lane goes past the Mansion House on the left, a well-proportioned house of the early 18th century. Continue down the narrow lane to a sharp left-hand bend. On the right is the entrance to a house, the gate next to it leads on to a grass track. Go down this to a hunting gate. You will come to this gate on the way back.

From the gate go up the opposite side of the valley on a faint grass track towards a house. There is a stile in the wall to the left of a field gate. On the lane beyond, continue for 300 yards up to a left-hand bend just past Nashend Farm. In front is a small gate on the right of a field gate. Go through on to a fenced path which ends with another small gate. From here keep straight ahead to a stile in the middle of the end hedge. Standing just inside the next field you can see a track going up and then through the hedge on the far side of the field. Pass the old cottage to go up this track and continue through the next field with the hedge on the right. In the far corner go over a stile, along a narrow path and so down on to Fidges Lane. Cross the lane and the grass bank and walk along the

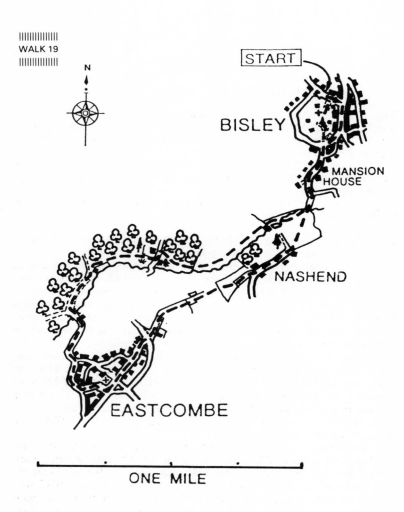

WALK 19

N

START

BISLEY

MANSION
HOUSE

NASHEND

EASTCOMBE

ONE MILE

narrow lane ahead. This is the village of Eastcombe. A modern town planner's nightmare — its narrow lanes twist and turn on the hillside, going between houses which face in all directions. Continue up the lane to the Lamb inn.

Walk on along the road past the Baptist church and turn right down an opening at the side of the school playground. On reaching the narrow lane at the bottom, turn left and in 100 yards, at the road junction, bear right down the left of two lanes — both of which are 'unsuitable for motor vehicles'. Follow the lane down an exceedingly steep hill and cross the valley. On the far side of the bridge turn right along a good track up the valley, with a small stream flowing down a meadow on the right. At the first house bear right round the back of the buildings along a narrow path at the bottom of the wood. Continue up the valley and in ½ mile step through an old broken-down wall where once there must have been a stile and go between a garden hedge on the left and a wire fence. Step through a narrow gap in a wall on to a lane and turn left up the hill and in a few yards turn right opposite the end of the house on the left. Here a well-used path goes into the wood and soon goes down to the line of the old path. At the end of the wood go over a stile and continue up the valley, keeping to the left of the chattering brook.

At a disused mill go over a stile and follow the garden wall to another stile with a small bridge. In the meadow beyond, turn left. The little 'wort', a 3 ft manhole cover brought all the way from London, is strangely out of place in the middle of this beautiful meadow. At the hunting gate in the corner, retrace your steps into Bisley.

When you get to the Seven Springs again, go up the long flight of steps at the side of the springs to the churchyard. Leave by the opening to the left of the lych gate. At the road turn left up the hill to the car.

EASTLEACH

WALK 20

★

7½ miles (12 km)

OS Landranger 163, Pathfinder SP 00/10, 20/30

This walk starts in one of the least spoilt villages on the Cotswolds and follows the valley of the river Leach. Eastleach lies 1 mile west of the Lechlade to Burford A361 road opposite Broughton Poggs and 1½ miles south of the A433 between Aldsworth and Burford. It is about 2 miles north-east of Fairford.

Cars can be parked along the road south from the church at Eastleach Martin. It is signposted to Southrop. GR: SP 202 049.

Eastleach, like so many villages in the Cotswolds, is divided into two parts, Eastleach Turville to the east of the river Leach and Eastleach Martin to the west. Each has its own church and they look at each other across the clear waters of the Leach. Two bridges unite the community — the road bridge with its old ford alongside and a picturesque clapper bridge. Cars still seem out of place in this village. The margin of the river as it flows between the bridges is most beautiful in April when a carpet of daffodils is in flower.

From the car walk along the lane to Eastleach Martin. Pass the church on the left and bear right. In 30 yards go over the crossroads and take the road to Broadwell and Holwell. This road passes the rectory on the right and goes along the valley with the stream on the left, the other side of a narrow field. Follow this lane for ¼ mile to the foot of Locombe Hill. As the road starts to rise up the hill bear left through a gate.

Keep to the main track, which is on a ledge on the side of the valley, as it follows the river upstream. The wide sweeps of the valley probably began during the Ice Age as the meanders of a larger stream. Over the years the water table has dropped and less and less water flows down. During a long dry period the stream bed may be dry. In nearly ½ mile at the wood turn left and walk next to the wall at the bottom of the wood. When the wood ends do not go through the gate in front but stay in the meadow and with a wall on the right go into the corner near the stream.

Now go into the field on the right and in 100 yards go through a gate into a meadow. From here a small gate can be seen at the far side of the next field, at the bottom of the wood next to the stream. Go through this gate and along the bottom of the wood on a path which winds between the trees. At a ruined wall, where the stream starts to sweep away to the left, turn right up and out of the wood. Walk along the bottom edge of

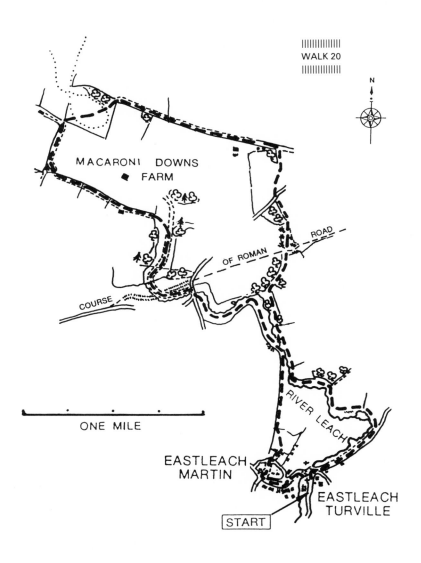

IIIIIIIIIIIII
WALK 20
IIIIIIIIIIIII

N

MACARONI DOWNS
FARM

OF ROMAN   ROAD

COURSE

ONE MILE

RIVER LEACH

EASTLEACH
MARTIN

EASTLEACH
TURVILLE

START

the field with an iron fence on the left, and continue up through a wood
to a cross-track.

This track follows approximately the line of the Roman Road now
called Akeman Street (Walk 16). It may have still been in use well into
the Saxon period and in places became distorted, as would seem to be
the case up to the right.

The Right of Way continues straight ahead through bushes. At the time of writing it is completely impassable in 100 yards. If it is waymarked with a blue arrow it will probably have been cleared, so walk on up the valley to emerge into a field. If there is no waymark turn right and on entering a field turn left with the scrub on your left.

Continue along the edge of the field next to a wood on the left as far as a road. Cross to a gate opposite and in the field beyond go to the right-hand corner of a wood. Continue to a road and turn left.

This road becomes a gated track and in ¾ mile passes a small group of trees on the left. This is marked on a 1912 map as 'Winter Pools (in ruins)'. Inside the enclosure there are slight earthworks. What comedies and tragedies were acted out here many years ago? In a further ¼ mile go through a gate and turn left up a bank. Go a few yards into the field and bear right, aiming a little to the left of some barn roofs seen above the orchard trees. Halfway across the field you will be able to see a gate in the corner.

As you go across the field you are crossing part of the long abandoned Bibury Race Course. It went in a rough figure of eight over to the right between the two pylons and behind the wood ¾ mile away.

At the track beyond the gate turn left and follow it for ¼ mile, to bear left in front of a small conifer plantation. Go through a gate and turn left along a track for ¾ mile, next to the wall on the left. Go down into a valley and join a good farm road. Continue over a cattle grid — look down and see how it is properly constructed with four hedgehog ramps.

In 200 yards there is a ford through the little River Leach on the right. This is the line of the Roman Road crossed earlier. It can be seen to go up to the right and from a little further round the bend it can be seen on the left as a shelf in the hillside.

On reaching the road turn right and in 30 yards, opposite the signpost to Hatherop, turn left through a gate to walk down the valley with the stream on your left. In ½ mile go through a gate and up a slope to another gate. Now keep ahead, with the wall on the right, for ½ mile. In the last field before Eastleach Turville bear slightly left to the end of a lane.

Go down the lane and at the T-junction turn right. In 20 yards turn left along a narrow path between low stone walls to a stone stile next to the car park of 'The Victoria' and so on to the road. Keep ahead down the grass slope and cross the road at the bottom. In front is a road to Southrop. From the beginning of this road another road goes to the left down through the quietest part of the village. Walk along here and in 200 yards pass a long, tall, blank wall, which is the back of a row of cottages. Only two new windows face the road, the other side is quite normal.

Follow the road round to the left and just before reaching the old houses on the left, turn right on the path which crosses the stream by the clapper bridge. Continue by the side of the clear water and go up through the churchyard to the road. Turn right back to the car.

DAGLINGWORTH

WALK 21

★

6 miles (9.5 km)

OS Landranger 163, Pathfinder SO 80/90

This walk is in Cirencester Park. On all gates leading into this estate there are notices which read 'Cirencester Park. You are welcome on foot and on horseback by permission of the Earl Bathurst. Dogs, Cars, Cycles or unaccompanied children are not allowed. Under Sec. 34(3) H.A. 1959. There is no public right of way over this land. Please do not damage trees, livestock or wildlife, no fires. Take your litter home.'

Daglingworth is 2½ miles from Cirencester and ½ mile west of the A417 (T) Gloucester to Cirencester road, from which it is signposted.

The walk starts 1 mile to the west of the village of Daglingworth. The following directions are from the east through the village. There is a maze of roads further west of the parking place and instructions from this direction would be very complicated.

Go through the village and follow the signposts to Sapperton and Stroud. In ¾ mile the road enters a wood and in a further ¼ mile there is a large clearing on the right. Cars may be parked here. GR: SO 974 046.

The magnificent Cirencester Park covers over 3000 acres on what was once land belonging to the Augustinian Abbey of Cirencester. In 1563 Queen Elizabeth sold the land to her physician, Sir John Denvers, and it later passed through various owners until in 1695 it was sold to the first Earl Bathurst. In 1718 the present house replaced one built by Sir Henry Pool some 50 years earlier. Meanwhile the laying-out of the park had started in 1704 and the basic outline was finished in 1735.

An early painting of Cirencester before the park was made shows the present private garden with large fields and open sheep pasture beyond. For many years the rows of small saplings must have looked strangely insignificant. Today the mature and well-tended woodlands provide one of the best examples of 18th century parkland in England and it is fortunate that the public may enjoy it.

Leave the car and walk through the back of the parking area into Overley Wood. In a few yards turn left along a track and in 300 yards come out on to Overley Ride. Turn left, cross the road and follow the wide grass ride for just over 1 mile to a meeting place of ten rides. Overley Ride, part of which you have walked, is 3 miles long. It starts near the tunnel entrance on Walk 22, Broad Ride starts 2 miles away to the west in Sapperton and ends over 3 miles to the east in Cirencester.

67

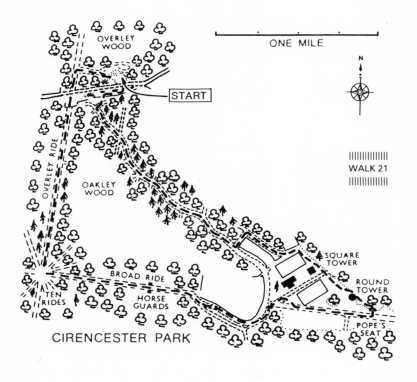

Turn left along Broad Ride. It will be seen that this ride is aligned, not on the house but on the tower of Cirencester parish church. In ¾ mile pass the two large sentry boxes, one on either side. This part is called 'Horse Guards'. Continue down to a fence across the ride. Go just to the right of this fence and follow the track along the narrow gully. In ¼ mile the track comes to an open space where three estate roads meet.

Continue on the estate road ahead and follow it up into the wood in front. In 300 yards look over to the left through an opening in the trees. This is the line of Broad Ride. Continue to the top of the hill and turn right at the kiosk along the stone track which soon bears left down the side of Broad Ride. On the left is Ivy Lodge with its impressive façade and beyond it, across the polo ground, is Square Tower. Follow the track for ½ mile to where it turns off to the right. Continue for ¼ mile to Pope's Seat — which looks like an elaborate 18th century bus shelter — named after the poet who was a friend of Lord Bathurst. He wrote an Epistle to Lord Bathurst in 1732, by which time the trees here were just becoming established.

It is possible to walk on into Cirencester some 2 miles away but if you do so, return to this point.

Continue the walk by going through the back of Pope's Seat, the path through the bushes will take you to the Round Tower. Keeping the wood on the right, cross the estate road and go past Square Tower to a track beyond the end of another polo ground. Turn left at the end of the fence to go down the side of the polo ground, passing two obstacles in the Cross Country Course. In 100 yards bear right to a track into a wood. Follow this track for ¼ mile to where it dips across the end of a small valley. Turn left here out of the wood and go downhill with a field on the left. In 200 yards the track goes down steeply into a valley. This is Haines Ash Bottom. Turn right.

Continue along Haines Ash Bottom, ignoring any paths or tracks which go up to the right or left. In 1 mile cross over a well-used estate road and go up the valley for a further ¼ mile to a small cross-track. Ahead, the main track bears round to the left. Here turn right and in 30 yards fork left. This path turns right in 150 yards and goes through bushes and small trees just outside the wood. In 100 yards look for an opening on the left and you will be able to see the parking place, where the walk started, just across the road.

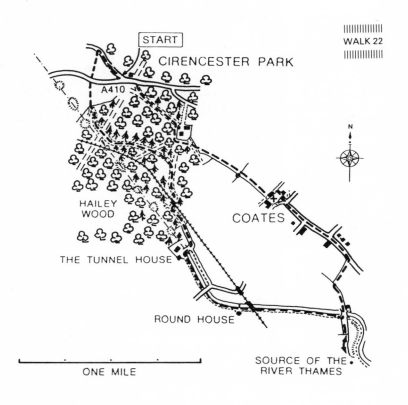

START

CIRENCESTER PARK

N

A410

HAILEY
WOOD

COATES

THE TUNNEL HOUSE

ROUND HOUSE

ONE MILE

SOURCE OF THE
RIVER THAMES

HAILEY WOOD

WALK 22

★

4½ miles (7 km)

OS Landranger 163, Pathfinder SO 80/90

This walk starts near one of the lodge gates of Cirencester Park and goes through estate woods and along an old canal towpath.

Cars can be parked on the grass verge of a lane which leaves the A419 Cirencester to Stroud road, 4 miles from Cirencester and 10 miles from Stroud. The lane is signposted to Sapperton and is 100 yards west of the Park Lodge. GR: SO 960 020.

A canal from the River Severn to Stroud was completed in 1779, mainly to ease the overland journey between Stroud and Bristol. At this time roads were very poor and the woollen industry, which was centred on Stroud, was flourishing. Efforts were then concentrated on improving communications between Stroud and London. The Thames and Severn Canal extended the first 8 miles of canal from the Severn to Stroud a further 29 miles to Lechlade, where it joined the Thames at the highest navigable point. It took 6½ years to build and cost about £250,000.

In its course up the Frome valley to Sapperton there are 28 locks, then comes the summit level 8 miles long — 2 of which are in a tunnel, followed by 15 locks to take it down to the Thames. The tunnel was built by working from both ends and by sinking shafts every few hundred yards along its course, so that the maximum number of men could be employed. There are spoil heaps above the tunnel to be seen in the fields and in the wood.

Walk along the lane towards Sapperton. On the right is Sapperton Park, an extension of Cirencester Park. In ¼ mile look on the left for a V stile in the wall. Beyond the stile go straight down the field to a gate on to the main A419 road. Cross with care and go through the gate opposite. Keep the same direction across the next field towards two gates close together on the edge of a wood. As you go across the field you will notice two of the spoil heaps, two large mounds, over to the right.

Enter the wood by the left of the two gates and bearing slightly left follow the main track. The soft surface at the side of the track, especially near the second cross-track, is an ideal place to find the footprints of animals, including deer, which live in the wood. At each cross-track go straight ahead and in ¾ mile pass under a railway bridge and then bear left. In 300 yards leave the wood and follow a track up to the eastern entrance of the tunnel.

71

Nearby is the Tunnel House inn, built to house the Cornish and Derbyshire miners working on the tunnel. It originally had three floors, the top was one large room, the middle had a few thin partitions and on the ground floor what is now the large lounge bar was the dining room. Outside there was a bowling alley, a vast stone water-cistern, stables and store sheds.

To continue the walk go down the slope by the side of the tunnel arch, lately restored to its former glory. In ½ mile the unusual round building by the side of the path is a watchman's house, built in 1790. The ground floor was a stable, the next two floors were living space and it was topped by a roof of lead to catch the rain water. It was very difficult to keep enough water in the 8 miles of the summit level so at times it was necessary to stop off parts. Opposite the round house the canal will be seen to narrow for a few yards. Here boards were dropped into grooves to keep the water level up in the tunnel. Boats would then come through but have to queue for as long as *ten weeks* while sufficient water accumulated in the next length to allow them to continue! Walk on down the towpath to the stone narrow-waisted bridge.

By turning right and walking ¼ mile pilgrims may visit a stone, erected by the Conservators of the river Thames, to mark the source of the river. Unfortunately no water has flowed from here for more than 50 years. The first visible flow is a mile down the valley. But it is a pleasant and well-trodden path.

From the old stone bridge over the canal, go to the stile and then up the hill, keeping next to the hedge on the right. In 200 yards, where the hedge curves round to the left, go over a stile on the right and follow the field boundary to the road. Turn left along the road and in ½ mile, where the road turns sharp right, go straight ahead along a narrow path between gardens to the churchyard. The walk continues to the farm-track beyond the churchyard. Turn left and in a few yards turn right just past a house on the right. Go up into a field, keeping the hedge on the left.

In about 300 yards, as the track begins to go down, there is a small pond on the left. This was once a dew-pond, and in this position it would have provided water for three fields, but with piped water on the farm it is no longer needed.

At the end of the field follow the waymarks into the wood and round the timber yard to the opposite side near the entrance. Here turn left along a grass ride. After 300 yards fork right to the main road which is only 50 yards away. Make sure the gate is secured after you have gone through, turn left and in 100 yards cross the road with care to the start of the walk.

WOODCHESTER

WALK 23

★

4 miles (6.5 km)

OS Landranger 162, Pathfinder SO 80/90

Little would be known of Woodchester in the outside world but for the fact that the largest Roman mosaic north of the Alps was discovered here in the late 18th century. The walk starts with a long climb from the Nailsworth Valley to Selsley Common, with the reward of good views, and ends with a gentle return.

Woodchester is on the A46 Bath to Stroud road, 2 miles south of Stroud.

The walk starts at the southern end of South Woodchester on a loop of old road now cut off from the A46. Park the car near the round tower opposite the entrance to Carr Tanning Co. Ltd. GR: SO 841 017.

Walk along the road towards the centre of South Woodchester, leaving the end of Convent Lane on your left. The round tower was a fine example of an early wool drying tower dating from the 17th century. It has lately grown a small extra round tower and turned into a house. It was connected with Frogmarsh Mill opposite which is now occupied by a firm dealing in leather. A mill was here in the reign of Charles I, though the main part of the buildings are mid 19th century. The long building next to the road has one of the earliest examples of weaver's windows in the Cotswolds. This type of window, with its row of long lights, can often be seen in the top floor of early mills — for example, the Piano Works in North Woodchester.

Continue along the road for ¼ mile into the village of South Woodchester. At the top of the rise turn sharp left up Bospin Lane. Keep to the steep lane until you reach the end where there is a stile on the right. In the field beyond there is a choice of two tracks. Take the right-hand one and with the wood on the right continue up the hill. Pass to the right of the cottage and follow a path next to the fence and wood on the right. Where the wood curves round to the right, keep straight on into the corner of the field where a stile takes you on to the corner of Selsley Common. Cross the road with care.

Near the notice about parking cars on the common is a concrete dew-pond — a square dish of concrete, now somewhat cracked but still collecting a little water. This method of watering stock on the high ground above the spring-line has been superseded by piped water and the drinking trough.

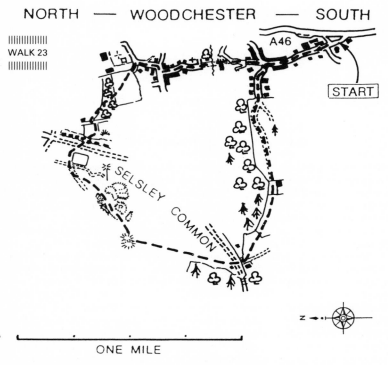

||||||||||||||
WALK 23
||||||||||||||

A46

START

SELSLEY COMMON

Z

ONE MILE

Strike off across the common, with first a wood on the left. Keep to the left-hand rim and go towards a mound in the distance. The view to the left is across the Severn estuary to the Forest of Dean beyond. The mound is a chambered long barrow and could be up to 5000 years old. It is known as 'The Toots' (toot, tump, barp and law are some of the regional names given to round barrows), from its remains looking like two round barrows. The gash in the middle was made by treasure hunters long ago.

From here walk on round the hill to a group of disused quarries. In the second one it used to be possible to find fossils but the rock-faces have been covered and are now grassed over. You may be lucky. When opposite the slender transmitting mast on the right, look down the common for a sunken grass track and then follow it down to the right. On reaching the track up to the mast go across and follow the wall on the right. At the end of the wall look over the main road (B4006) at the houses. There is a stile next to the garden wall of the fifth house from the left. Go down the track to the house and continue to the stile. From here it is just possible to see the stile down in the opposite corner — but to reach it, walk along the field to the right and then turn left next to the bushes. The right of way is following old field boundaries, the ridge

74

across the field is one. Beyond the stile is a sunken lane and another stile, a little to the left. In the next field bear right next to the fence and in 100 yards go over a stone stile incorporated in the fence. Follow the path down through the wood and cross the next field to the far left-hand corner. This leads to a walled track and a T-junction with a lane.

A small diversion to the left takes you to the churchyard and ruins of the old parish church, abandoned in 1863. All that remains is a Norman chancel arch and doorway and a perpendicular window. On entering the churchyard a square flat area of grass, clear of tombs, can be seen on the left. It was in the graveyard here that the great pavement of a Roman villa was found about 4 ft below the surface. Burials damaged parts of the pavement but much of it is still intact. This mosaic was the floor of a hall measuring nearly 49 ft sq and part of a suite of rooms enclosing a courtyard or garden — in all about 200 ft sq. Another group of large buildings, probably the farm unit and workers' accommodation, is known to have existed on the south side. The mosaic used to be uncovered every ten years. Unfortunately it was found to be deteriorating so it has not been on show since 1973. A portable replica of the pavement has been made and is on show from time to time.

Return along the lane, past the walled track you came along and up the slope into North Woodchester. At the T-junction turn right and in 50 yards left to go past the Royal Oak Inn. In 300 yards, after passing the church, go ahead to the footpath sign and follow the metalled path down the hill. At the entrance to the house on the opposite side of the valley go straight ahead to join a lane. Keep the same direction along a quiet lane and in 100 yards you are back at the bottom of Bospin Lane.

Continue along the road to Frogmarsh Mill and the car.

MINCHINHAMPTON

WALK 24

★

4½ miles (7 km)

OS Landranger 162, Pathfinder SO 80/90

This is a walk which can be undertaken after wet weather as it avoids places where there could be mud. Although it is almost level there are views across neighbouring valleys and the Vale of Gloucester.

Minchinhampton is 3 miles south of Stroud set high on the hill overlooking the Frome and Nailsworth valleys.

Cars can be parked in the car park behind the Market Hall in Friday Street. GR: SO 873 007.

Minchinhampton has a long history — 4000 years is a conservative estimate. Some of the early settlement will be seen on the common where it has not been disturbed by later development. In the 13th century the town almost achieved the status of a borough. It certainly had its own market and a five-day fair. Like Winchcombe in the North Cotswolds it was a leading cloth manufacturing town until the 18th century. The craftsman, working in his own home, controlled the method of production which often involved all the family as well as apprentices and paid assistants.

By 1740 the demand for cloth was increasing at such a pace that the cost of wool began to rise, especially with the introduction of softer foreign wools. Consequently the smaller units could not find the capital to purchase bulk supplies from distant importers. So grew up the big businessman who could finance the purchase of both new material and finished product and who soon found that the new machinery would operate faster and cheaper than the craftsman. At this time Minchinhampton moved into the twilight of the cloth trade — the centres now being the valleys where waterpower was all important. The dawn of the 19th century saw Minchinhampton becoming a commuter town when its weavers were forced to go down the hill to work in the new factories. As a commuter town it has remained, though now the families leave to work in chemical or plastics factories.

Walk along Bell Lane, opposite the Market Hall, with the church on the right. The small building on the left has a good example of medieval ecclesiastical lettering, which is thought to be unique. Follow the boundary of the churchyard round to the right to an opening on to the common. Turn left along the edge of the common and follow the wall on the left round to a road. Cross the road and walk along the top of a ridge. This is called 'The Bulwarks' and archaeologists are not sure what its

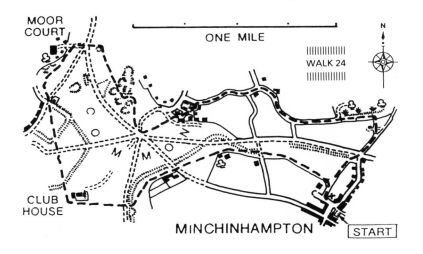

purpose was but it is older than the Celtic Fort you pass through later. In 200 yards leave the ridge and bear left past the entrance to Seymour House and Westfield. This house gets its name from the large medieval field which stretched from Minchinhampton out to here. When the wall turns left continue across the common to the right of the house and trees in front. Over much of the common there is a golf course so keep a wary eye for golfers 'addressing the ball'. The walk crosses fairways a number of times.

Cross the road and go past Windmill House. Now follow the Bulwarks for ¼ mile to where it is destroyed by quarrying, next to the road. Bear right across the road and go to the left of a group of houses in the trees some 300 yards away. These are connected with the golf course. The view to the left is up the Nailsworth valley to Avening (Walk 27).

Pass the end wall, which has a large white cross on it, and just beyond turn right past the club house. Now aim for the wayside cross, standing in a gap ½ mile away. The view to the left is now of the tree-filled valley of Woodchester Park.

After crossing the road go through a gap in the Iron Age fortifications. The view from here is over South Woodchester (Walk 23).

Now bear right towards the wayside cross which is a war memorial. Continue out to the edge of the common. The view is now over the Severn valley. The hill in the distance which has a tuft of trees on top is May Hill, a famous landmark seen from Gloucestershire, Herefordshire and Worcestershire.

Walk to the right along the common to the road junction at the entrance to Moor Court. Cross the main road from Stroud to Minchinhampton and go ahead for 100 yards to a small round pond in a hollow. This is a well preserved dew-pond, there being no natural

77

supply of water for animals on the common. Here turn right towards some mounds and hollows in which a few thorn trees grow. These are old quarry workings. After the quarries bear right to the crossroads. This place is called 'Tom Longs Post' and is said to be the place where highwaymen, who took their own lives to escape capture, were buried.

Turn left downhill towards Burleigh. Leave the road away to the left and go to the right of a metal cattle drinking trough. Go down a narrow strip of common near the house which shows only its blank gable-end. At the bottom of the slope turn right along a rough road which soon becomes a narrow path. Turn left at the T-junction and go down the path between walls. Just past the first house on the left look through the gap in the wall at the old well-head. How many hours used people to spend toiling to get the basic needs of life which we take so much for granted?

At the lane turn right. In 300 yards there is a gate in the tall wall on the right. The right-hand stone gate-post must be at least 10 ft long. His brother must have been broken some time — children should be asked to find it! Continue along the lane and at the junction keep straight ahead past Burleigh House on the right and Burleigh Farm on the left. Walk along the lane called Lovers Lane.

Continue along the lane keeping the same direction. In 200 yards, just past a footpath sign, the house on the left is called the Old Weavers House. On reaching Besbury Common (which is National Trust land) bear right along the top of the common with the wall on the right. The view from here is across the Golden Valley and up the wooded Toadsmoor Valley and Bisley (Walk 19).

Pass two stiles and at the footpath sign turn right through a V stile into a field. Follow the fence on the right past a house to cross a drive and, at the far end of a small paddock, an interesting metal step-stile on to a lane. Go along the lane to the main road, bear right and cross to the grass. With the wall on the left, walk to the entrance to the common near the churchyard. Retrace the 300 yards back to the car.

Did you notice the 'scale of charges' set high on the end wall of the Market Hall?

STINCHCOMBE HILL

WALK 25

★

3½ miles (5.5 km)

OS Landranger 162, Pathfinder ST 69/79

On this walk the panorama can hardly be surpassed anywhere in the British Isles. Choose a day when the visibility is good and a map will help to identify some of the places seen.

Stinchcombe Hill overlooks Dursley which is 2 miles from the M5, 11 miles from Gloucester and 18 miles from Bristol. The hill is reached by two lanes. The steeper one leaves the centre of Dursley opposite the post office. It starts as May Lane, then becomes The Hill Road and near the top of the hill it is The Broadway. The other approach is from the A4135 Tetbury road, a mile from the centre of Dursley. Here a lane is signposted 'Stinchcombe Hill and Golf Course'. On reaching the open land go along the unfenced narrow road, with the golf club house away on the right, to a large well-made car park. GR: ST 743 984.

Stinchcombe Hill was given for the use of the public by Sir Stanley William Tubbs.

From the car park walk back parallel to the road you have just come along. Keep to the edge of the grass area, just above the wood on the hillside. The view is down towards Stancombe Park. On reaching the corner turn left along the service road, to cut across the corner where you came in. This will bring you to the club house. Continue in the same direction across a tongue of common towards some sheds under the trees ¼ mile away. A short way beyond the sheds bear right on a well-worn path though scrub, just below the rough grass on the left where the golfers try not to go. The view to the right is over Dursley to Cam Long Down and Coaley Park .

When the path ahead can be seen to go downhill through the trees, turn left along a path just below the golf course. This path goes all round the hill, keeping away from the golfers but with periodic clearings in the trees for magnificent views — and at these places there is usually a seat provided.

In ¼ mile the path passes a footpath sign pointing down to Woodfield and then a house in the trees. Just past here, at the end of a small wood, turn right on a bridlepath which comes from the car park over to the left and goes to the right through old quarry workings. This path goes down the hill to Stinchcombe Village.

At the raised golf tee on the left, turn round a stone sticking up out of the grass and go along a mown path. When the mown path bears left up

WALK 25

N

SHELTER

STINCHCOMBE HILL

CAR PARK

START

GOLF CLUBHOUSE

ONE MILE

to a tee, go straight ahead to follow a well-trodden path round the back of the tee. For the next ¼ mile the path is just below the level of a fairway, giving a worm's eye view of the golfers as they earnestly trudge along with their trolleys.

At various places along this path it is possible to see some of the layers of rock which make up the hill. Careful examination of these will reveal many small fossils. Long before man, or even animals, lived on this earth the Cotswolds stretched much further west — some believe as far as Ireland. The pushing up of the western side and then the gradual wearing away has revealed what was once at the bottom of the sea. The fossils here come from the Mesozoic period — from 65 to 225 million years ago. Some lumps of rock are the graveyards of dozens of shells (mostly Brachiopods) about the size of a hazel nut. The best specimens can be removed complete by carefully picking round them with a needle or a sharp nail.

Continue along the path to the shelter, and if the wind is strong, stay here for a while and study the view. If it is a calm day the best view is from the second seat a little further on round the hill or from the Ordnance Survey pillar just behind it. If you have O.S. Landranger Sheet No. 162 the shelter is the small black dot under the 'e' in Stinchcombe. (Map Reference 736984.) The view to your right is up the Severn valley between the outlyers of the North Cotswolds and the Malvern Hills to the Black Country. To your left the view is over the Bristol Channel to Exmoor, and in front to the mountains of Wales. At your feet is the patchwork of fields on both sides of the motorway and beyond the winding Severn are the low hills of the Forest of Dean. To 'set' any map, look across the river for the town of Lydney on the hillside. Line up Lydney with Stinchcombe Hill on the map and point the line at Lydney across the valley. Places on the ground should now be in the same direction as they are from Stinchcombe Hill on the map.

To return to the car, go over the other side of the hill and follow the paths out on to a tongue of land. The car park can be seen nearly ½ mile away to the left. Turn left down the track which goes round the hillside and back to the car park.

OWLPEN

WALK 26

★

3½ miles (5.5 km)

OS Landranger 162, Pathfinder ST 69/79

This walk is for those who like a good climb — at one place an average of 1 in 5 for ¼ mile — and to be rewarded by superb views.

Uley is 2 miles east of Dursley at the head of a short valley. It is on the B4066 road between Dursley and Stroud. In the early 19th century Uley was renowned throughout Europe for its blue cloth.

The walk starts at the very small hamlet of Owlpen, ½ mile east of Uley. Do not approach Owlpen from the hills, for the lane is very steep and narrow, and by no means straight. Go to Uley and leave the main road through the village just above the church, where there is a small village green. It is signposted to Owlpen. Cars can be parked 50 yards past the Manor House. GR: ST 797 983.

The hamlet of Owlpen consists of a church, an old mill and an Elizabethan manor house though the parish stretches for over a mile in both directions along the wooded hillside. With your back to the church go over the stile on the right of the gate and follow the footpath sign to 'Stoutshill' and keep near to the hedge on the right.

Just beyond the stile into the next field look over to the right at the rough ground in the adjoining field. This was once a reservoir discharging water into the leats of a mill down the valley. For over 100 years, after the mill was closed, the area lapsed into a tree-covered wetland and though somewhat reduced in size, has now returned to a reservoir. Originally water was fed into two leats, one on either side of the valley. The nearest one is followed down through two more fields. In the first field is an attractive 18th century stone bridge, you will come back over this. Beyond the stile at the end of the second field turn right to another stile and go down the slope.

In this narrow valley, between the gate behind and the old houses in front, there was once one of the largest mills in Gloucestershire. It was called Shepherd's Mill. The building on the right, which is now a dwelling, used to be the scouring house, one of some 30 which filled the valley. The cottages in front on the bank were the press shop and the clerk's house is over to the right. Shepherd and Hicks had bought a small mill on the site in 1789 and greatly enlarged it, only to become bankrupt in 1837. The demand for broadcloth fluctuated. During wartime there was a great demand for 'Stroud Scarlet and Uley Blue', when every soldier dressed like Her Majesty's guardsmen, whose

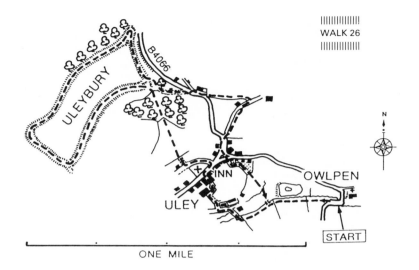

ONE MILE

uniform is still made in the Cotswolds (as are billiard table and tennis ball covers and other high class material). Did the great mill owners strive to enter the ranks of the gentry instead of putting more of their immense profits back into their industry? Edward Shepherd built Gatcombe Park (Walk 27).

As you go up the slope beyond you can wonder how many men, women and children have climbed the same track up to Uley after a 14-hour day in the 'new' factory.

Where the track joins the road continue ahead to the end of the pavement in front of the new houses and turn right up a good surfaced path. At the old school buildings turn right and at the road turn left. This leads to the main road in Uley just below the church. Cross the road and go up to the end of the churchyard. Here turn left and follow the footpath sign to 'Uleybury'. In 100 yards, just before the first house on the right, turn right and go up a narrow path to a stile. Climb up the field in front, bearing very slightly to the left, to the highest corner of the field where there is a hunting gate leading into the wood. Go over the stile on the right of this gate and continue up through the wood with an old sunken trackway down below on the left. On nearing the top of the wood bear left up to a stile. The mounds beyond here are the remains of the complicated main entrance to the hill fort of Uleybury.

Turn left up a steep track which goes to the rampart and the silted ditch which is now a level cartway. Continue round the hill fort in a clockwise direction. The wall on the right encloses about 32 acres and the circuit is 1¼ miles. As the fortifications curve round the hillside there is a good view down over Uley to Owlpen and the wooded hills beyond. After the first corner the hill standing alone in the valley is

Downham Hill, and after the second corner the valley is broken up by Cam Long Down, a popular place to walk over. At the third corner turn right and just before the fourth corner bear left and go down through the old entrance gate.

Do not go over the stile in front — that is the way you came up to the fort but bear left with a hedge on the left and a fence on the right. The path soon descends the hillside as a sunken track. On reaching the main road turn right. Keep to the right of the road until you are just past the entrance to 'The Grove', then cross to the footway on the other side. Turn left just past the house near the bend and go down a track. In 10 yards go over a stile on the right. Continue down the field towards Mutterall Farm keeping a few yards from the hedge on the right to the first of two gates. On the lane beyond turn right. Walk up the lane for 100 yards and opposite a cottage turn left over a fence. The right of way continues up the field next to the hedge on the right to a gate. A field-path running parallel to a track was common in the days when some tracks were so muddy that only horses could manage them.

On reaching the main road cross to the footway and in 100 yards cross back again onto the village green. Go straight across the green to the houses opposite and down a gravel path between two houses; the left-hand one is set back and has had its ground floor converted into two garages. Follow the red brick wall on the right round to the left. Here the old road goes along the end of the gardens of the houses on the left. In 30 yards bear right down a path, with a hedge on the right and a garden fence on the left to a stile. Go straight ahead down the field to a gate and footbridge. In the next field bear slightly right up to a stile. This is one end of the attractive footbridge passed on the way out. Cross the bridge and turn left, to retrace the 300 yards back to the car.

AVENING

WALK 27

★

4½ miles (7 km)

OS Landranger 162, Pathfinder ST 89/99

The village of Avening nestles in a well-wooded valley surrounded by bare and windswept hills. This walk rises gently to the top of one of these hills and returns through woodland. Avening is on the A434 halfway between Nailsworth and Tetbury. Cars can be parked on the quiet road near the school at the Nailsworth or lower end of the village. Turn off the main road 10 yards below the Bell Inn. GR: ST 880 980.

In the early 19th century Avening had a number of mills. The oldest, called Avening Mill, dates back to the 17th century and was 300 yards upstream from the start of the walk. It was first a fulling mill and later a cloth mill. George's Mill has been demolished but it stood on the other side of the main road from the school, in the field opposite the coal merchant's house. The largest mill was Longford's, a mile downstream.

Overlooking Avening from the north is Gatcombe Park. It was built by Edward Shepherd who had one of the largest mills in Gloucestershire at Uley (Walk 26). Cobbett, in his *Rural Rides*, describes Gatcombe Park as having '. . . one of the finest, most magnificent woods, of 200 acres I dare say . . . going from a valley up a gently rising hill'. The wood is still there today but the Shepherds and their mill have long since gone. Today the house is owned by Princess Anne.

Leave the road by the school and go up the path between walls at the side of the church. The next ¼ mile is a 'study in stiles'. The two fields have become many small paddocks, each fence having a stile with its own personality. The path is well waymarked and walked so the word stile has not been repeated ten times. Go into a field and continue round the hillside. Down on the right in the marsh is a large clump of reedmace surrounded by a wire fence. Bear slightly left, rising slowly, to the opposite corner of the field to the right of a house.

In the next field turn left up to a lane. Turn right and follow the lane, passing a turning to the farm on the left where the damp verges are covered with butterbur — the cluster of pink heads, some male and some female, are rich in nectar and a boon to beekeepers. The flowers are followed by large rhubarb-like leaves. At the barn on the left, fork left and follow the track to a gate.

Just beyond the gate there is a ford from which water flows away through two small openings in the wall on the left. Cross the stone

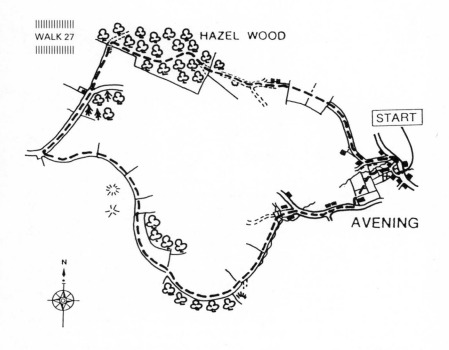

causeway on the right into the field and bear left along the bottom of the field.

Continue up the valley with a wall or hedge on the left for over 1 mile. At the stile at the top of the hill look over to the left to a grassy mound. This is a long barrow dating back nearly 5000 years. Continue along the path with first a wall and then a hedge on the left for nearly ½ mile to a gate on to a track. Here is the meeting of ways.

Turn right along the track. Within the next 200 yards the hedge on the left is made up of at least 13 different plants. See if you can recognise them — sloe, hazel, ash, traveller's joy (or old man's beard), maple, hawthorn, rose, bramble, wych-elm, beech, dogwood, elderberry and sycamore. In a further 200 yards, where there is a stone building in the corner of the field on the left, the track bears right. Go through the gate in front and then along the edge of a cultivated field, having the wall on the left.

At the far end of the wall go down a sunken track and through a gate. Just inside the wood leave the main track and turn right along a path just inside the wood. In 200 yards go straight over a cross-path and into the wood. This is called Hazel Wood and some of the old hazel trees can be seen. They were regularly cut down to the ground when they had grown a dozen or so long shoots; this is called coppicing.

86

Follow the path to the end of the wood. Go through the farm gate and follow the track down through the field. Pass in front of the farm buildings and go through a gate in the corner of the field at the end of the garden wall.

The path continues almost level across two fields. From these fields you can see Gatcombe Park across the valley to the left. (For early history of Gatcombe Park see Walk 26.)

The gate ahead leads to a track with a wall on the left and a hedge on the right. The rough track gradually improves as it bears left down to the main road, where a right turn will soon bring you back to the car.

BAGPATH

WALK 28

★

6 miles (9.5 km)

OS Landranger 162, Pathfinder ST 69/79, 89/99

This walk is up one well-wooded valley and down another, mostly through parkland. After very wet weather the lower parts of the valley may become muddy.

Bagpath is a small village ½ mile south of the A4135 Dursley to Tetbury road. It is signposted 3 miles from Dursley and 5 miles from Tetbury. At the crossroads, high above the village, take the turning to 'Scrubbett's Farm'. This is signposted a short way along as 'No through road', but continue for nearly 1 mile. Cars can be parked on the grass verge just past the solitary house on the right which was once a lodge to Ozleworth Park. GR: ST 897 936. The stone pillars at the entrance to the drive are still there, and the walk ends by coming through them.

Walk on along the road and down the hill. In front, across the valley, there is a fine view of Boxwell Court, so named from 40 acres of box trees planted nearby. Just beyond a sharp left-hand bend is the entrance to Scrubbett's Farm with its tennis courts. Here the road suddenly becomes a track. Most of the Cotswolds by-roads were like this until 100 years ago, making communications very difficult. Follow this old road down the hill and, just before it crosses the bottom of the valley, look on the left for two stone gate posts with a broken iron gate. Go through the gate and follow the path through tall trees standing in a carpet of wild garlic (ramsons). Keeping the stream on the right continue up the valley ½ mile. The path forks, so bear right and continue up the right-hand side of the valley past a lake which is now little more than a swamp, with enormous bamboo bushes along its edge.

Cross back to the left of the stream and go through a gate at the end of the wood. This leads to grassland in which a faint track can be seen ahead leading to a gate and rising slowly out of the valley to sweep round the front of Lasborough Park. Cross the drive some 50 yards to the right of the garden gate and go up the hill opposite, aiming slightly to the right of the end of the wood on the skyline. On reaching the top of the rise keep the same direction along the side of the valley to a wicket gate seen in the wall 300 yards ahead. Across the valley on the opposite slope is the small hamlet of Lasborough. Beyond the gate keep to the wall on the left and pass to the left of the 'Castle Mound'. Continue round the mound, down to a gate on to the road and turn left past the church. The

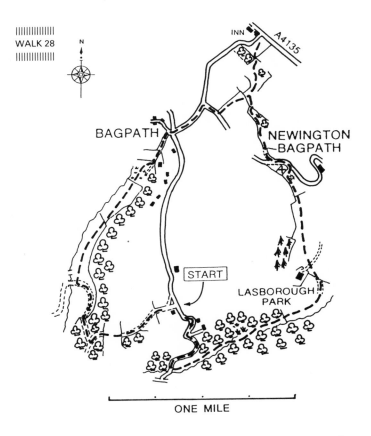

WALK 28

ONE MILE

two men said to be the last to be hanged for highway robbery in England are buried in this churchyard. A few yards past the church bear right over a stile next to a gate. Follow the wall on the right to a gate leading on to a track with a wall on the left and a wood down to the right. At the end of the wood the track leads round to a gate. In the field turn left. Those wishing to return direct to the car should not go through the gate but turn left to the corner of the field and miss the next paragraph.

Those wishing to visit the inn should turn right and go up the field. In 200 yards a small group of trees next to the path are worth noting as they are glean or wild cherry. Now bear right up the side of the valley to the right of a wood where there is a gate into a field. Continue in the field beyond to the far corner next to the Hunters Hall. To continue the walk retrace your steps to the bottom of the long field.

The short lengths of wall which make the corner of the field were repaired a few years ago and the stile was removed. Climb over the wall and step over the narrow stream where it comes out from under one of the walls. There is a faint track leading up the slope to the right-hand hedge near the skyline. Follow this and then keep near the hedge to a gate and on to a lane. Turn right and in 200 yards turn left at the T-junction, and continue to the crossroads above Bagpath.

Take the road in front which goes downhill to the right, but in 10 yards turn left down a narrow track between walls. After 100 yards keep near the garden wall on the left through one field and into a second. Now turn right keeping near the hedge for a few yards, then bear left following a track down and round the hill. Do not be tempted along an obvious and inviting glade to the left, the right of way is further down to the right. From this side of the valley it is possible to look across at the much steeper side opposite, where the fields look as if they have steps all down the hillside. These are caused by the soil slowly 'creeping' down. Further down the valley great wedges of the hillside have 'slumped' down towards the stream, which is steadily carrying the soil out to the Bristol Channel.

Continue down the valley for ½ mile to an old stone bridge which was part of the carriageway to Ozleworth Park, just over the hill on the right. Turn left at this cross-track and go into a wood. In a further 100 yards turn left up through the wood to a gate into a field. Straight ahead across the field, to the left of a clump of trees, is a gate which leads on to a track. Follow this track for nearly ½ mile until it goes between stone pillars on to the lane near the start of the walk.

WOTTON-UNDER-EDGE

WALK 29

★

5 miles (8 km)

OS Landranger 162, Pathfinder ST 69/79

This walk is to the Tyndale Monument and is mainly through National Trust woodland. There are wonderful views from the monument. Wotton-under-Edge lies under the foot of the escarpment and is 3 miles from Dursley. It is 17 miles north from Bristol and 8 miles west of Tetbury.

Cars may be parked in the large car park on the old market, still called 'The Chipping', near the centre of the town. It is well signposted. GR: ST 757 931.

Wotton reached its highest peak of prosperity between 1600 and 1850. The shortage of water prevented the expansion which other towns achieved in the 19th century. It is a town the character of which has not been changed by a diet of concrete and is therefore worth exploring. A notable inhabitant was Isaac Pitman, who was appointed head of the Free Church School in 1836 — but only for ten months, when he was dismissed for 'his unscriptural views displeasing to the Committee'. In the next year he started a school of his own — and developed his famous system of shorthand.

Leave the car park near the old fire station and go to the main shopping street. Turn left and at the crossroads turn right. At the next crossroads go up Tabernacle Pitch ahead. At the top is Roland Hill's Tabernacle, rebuilt in 1850 in hard grey stone.

At the top turn left and in 200 yards, when the road narrows, keep straight ahead up a narrow track. This bridlepath goes up to a lane called London Lane. Turn right and follow the lane up the hill to the top, where there is a footpath sign to the Tyndale Monument on the left. Go along this path between hedges for 100 yards to the beginning of Westridge Wood. The Cotswold Way, a long-distance walk of 100 miles between Chipping Campden and Bath, comes across the field from the left to this gate. It is waymarked with a white dot and a yellow (footpath) or blue (bridleway) arrow painted on posts or trees. You will follow the Cotswold Way for the next 2 miles.

Go along the track ahead with the hedge on the right to a cross-track. Remember this place as you will come back to it and turn up the track on the right. Now go straight across and in 300 yards go straight over the next cross-track. In 50 yards bear right along a smaller path. This goes round the outside of the fortifications of Brackenbury Camp. At the

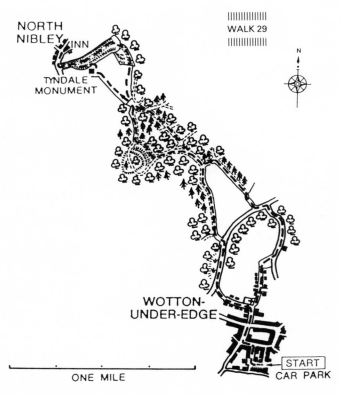

NORTH
NIBLEY INN

TYNDALE
MONUMENT

WOTTON-
UNDER-EDGE

START
CAR PARK

ONE MILE

junction of tracks bear right, following the arrow. In 300 yards at a
clearing, bear round to the left to a gate under tall trees. Remember this
gate because you will come to it on the way back. Go through the gate
and at the end of the trees bear left near to the fence on the left.

The monument commemorates William Tyndale. He was born in the
last years of the 15th century, probably at Stinchcombe, and after going
to Oxford was tutor to the children of Sir John Walsh at Little Sodbury.
He was a fierce opponent of Medievalism and in 1524 found it safer to
go to Germany to translate the Bible into English. He never returned to
England. His translation of the New Testament was completed in 1526.
The first books of the Old Testament were finished and sent to England
for printing in 1529 but they were shipwrecked and lost. However, by
the end of 1530 they were re-translated and this time arrived safely. He
suffered martyrdom by burning in 1536. At times Tyndale's Bible is
more vivid than the authorised version, which follows it closely. This is
part of Genesis — 'But the serpent was sotyller than all the beastes of the
felde which ye LORDE God had made and sayd vnto the woman. Ah syr
that God hath sayd ye shall not eate of all maner trees in the garden. . . .

92

Then sayd the serpent vnto the woman: tush ye shall not dye. . . .'

Those who do not wish to continue to North Nibley should retrace their steps down the field to the gate under tall trees and miss the next paragraph.

Those wishing to go into North Nibley go to the right at the back of the Monument down to a stile in the hedge. The path goes down the steep side of the hill by steps to a track in a deep cutting. Continue out to the road and turn right into North Nibley. To return to Wotton retrace your steps to the track in the deep cutting. Walk up the track to the gate at the top and follow the track beyond through the edge of an old quarry and across the field to the drinking troughs. Keep straight on to the gate under tall trees.

Go straight ahead from the gate across the clearing to a well-used path which rises and joins a track. A few yards up this track bear right up a path. Follow this track for 300 yards and when it forks go right. At the first cross-track keep straight ahead. At the second cross-track look carefully for a narrow path opposite. Go along this path and in 100 yards continue on the track.

At the cross-track passed on the way out, turn left, with a hedge and field on the right. In 100 yards at a cross-track turn right. This track continues for ½ mile to a road. Turn left and in a few yards go down a lane to the right which is not signposted. In ¼ mile, a little way past a house on the left, turn right at the end of a little garden to go over a stile next to a gate. From here you will see away to the right some medieval strip-lynchetts. The steep banks which form the lower edge of the long narrow fields run round the hillside. Some have hedges on them but others have become smooth slopes in the grass fields.

Go down the field and at the bottom bear left to the beginning of a path between old hedges. Continue past the new houses and up the lane to the top of Tabernacle Pitch. Go down to the Gloucester road, cross over and in 100 yards turn left down the main shopping street. Take the first turning back to the car park.

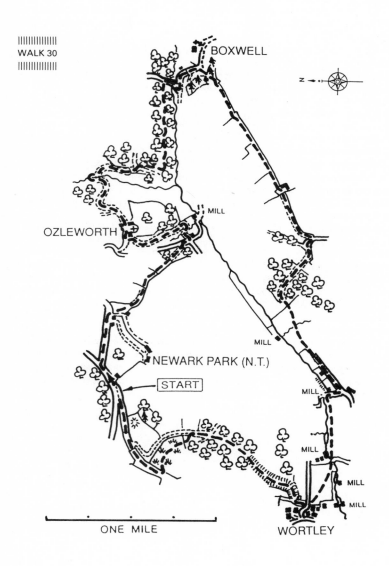

WALK 30

BOXWELL

N

OZLEWORTH

MILL

MILL

NEWARK PARK (N.T.)

START

MILL

MILL

MILL

MILL

MILL

ONE MILE

WORTLEY

OZLEWORTH

WALK 30

★

9 miles (14.5 km)

OS Landranger 162, Pathfinder ST 69/79, 89/99

This walk visits isolated valleys, open hill tops and two 18th century parks, Ozleworth and Boxwell.

Cars may be parked on the wide grass verge of a lane ½ mile east of Wotton-under-Edge at the top of the hill. GR: ST 778 934. It may also be reached from the junction of the B4058 and the A4153 2 miles from Dursley. The lane signposted Ozleworth goes from this junction. Do not take any turning to the left along this lane. The Post Office Tower, not far from the start, is a smaller edition of the one in London.

Walk along the lane away from the hill down to Wotton-under-Edge, past the park wall and turn right to go down to the entrance to Newark Park (National Trust property). 50 yards past the main entrance there is a footpath sign pointing into a field; follow its direction diagonally down to the bottom corner. Beyond the stile follow what was once an old road for ½ mile down to a lane. Turn right and in a few yards, at the entrance to Ozleworth Park, turn left through the gate.

Pass the lodge and follow the track across the valley round to a gate at the bottom of a wood. Continue up to the left of the wood to emerge at the side of the lawn at Ozleworth Park. The right-hand side is the original 18th century house, with a Regency front, having a porte-cochère (large covered porch) added later. Turn right and go along the road into the courtyard. The church, which is now redundant, has a rare hexagonal tower which is said to date from the time of Roger Berkley who died in 1131. Much 13th and 14th century work has survived the 19th century restoration. The building is set in a circular churchyard.

Continue the walk by going through the archway and following the track. As you go downhill do not fork left but go down and round to an old bridge, now unsafe. This was the entrance drive from the east. Go past the bridge for 100 yards and cross the stream by a new bridge and return on the other side. Now follow the old drive to below the wood and then into the wood.

Climb up to a cross-track. Turn right downhill for 50 yards and then bear left on to a less pronounced path which goes between the trees along the side of the hill. In ¾ mile the path emerges onto a walled track coming down from the left. Turn right down this ancient and long disused road across the valley and up to a T-junction. Here turn left and climb up to a fine view of Boxwell Court — so named from the extensive woods of box trees in this secluded valley. When the track turns left round a high wall bear right up to a conifer plantation. Go through a small gate and follow the path through the trees to a wide gap at the top. Beyond here follow first a hedge and then a wall on the left for over ¾ mile. From these fields there are fine views over the valley to Ozleworth and Newark Parks and to the long line of woodland on the skyline where the walk started.

At the farm buildings maintain the same direction along the farm track to a T-junction and turn right. In 100 yards fork left down a track which curves round to the right and enters a wood. Follow the concrete road downhill and when it emerges at the bottom go straight ahead through a gate. Down to the right is the disused Hell Mill which had one of the longest leats in the county, stretching almost ½ mile upstream. The mill was well established by the late 17th century. From the gate cross the field to another gate and then keep the same direction over the brow of the hill to a track past Whitehall Farm — a good look at the garden is rewarding. In a further ¼ mile turn right down a good track to a ruined mill. This was Nowell's; some of the stonework can still be seen on the right. On the left is a stile leading to a footpath down the valley next to the stream. Go down here and in ¼ mile look in the trees on the right where ivy-covered ruins of a tall building can be seen. This is all that is left of Monk's Mill. It was recorded in 1604 but must have been started long before that. It changed hands a number of times and grew to be very large. By the mid 19th century it consisted of a long four storey building with a three storey extension and numerous outbuildings. After the next stile you are on the Cotswold Way, which will be followed back to the car. In the large square field which is crossed diagonally, aim for the electricity pole in the middle. Away to the left is yet another mill of the early 17th century; this one also had a dye-house. It is interesting to contemplate that this valley was a busy industrial centre at the time of Shakespeare.

On reaching the lane, cross to the gate opposite and follow the track beyond for 100 yards and look for a waymark on the right which leads to a sunken track. This is a good example of a hollow way which has been worn down through the soft rock. After climbing for 1 mile the track goes along next to a field on the right. When a wood can just be seen away to the right, look carefully on the left for a waymark sign. Here a narrow path will take you down to a stile and a view of the head of the valley. Walk round to a gate seen in the fence ahead. The view to the left is down the valley known as Nanny Farmer's Bottom. Beyond the gate turn right and with first the fence and then a wall on the right go to a gate. This takes you on to a track, at the other end of which is your car.